T0095631

CAREER REFLECTIONS
from inside a Corporate Giant
1964–1981

Experiences in
an American
Automobile Plant

JIM SARAFIN

authorHOUSE®

AuthorHouse™
1663 Liberty Drive
Bloomington, IN 47403
www.authorhouse.com
Phone: 1-800-839-8640

Published by AuthorHouse 6/7/2013

ISBN: 978-1-4817-2233-9 (sc)
ISBN: 978-1-4817-2232-2 (hc)
ISBN: 978-1-4817-2231-5 (e)

Library of Congress Control Number: 2013903783

Front cover illustration by Stephen Adams.

This book is printed on acid-free paper.

Table of Contents

Introduction:

EARLY LIFE EXPERIENCES AND THE ROAD TO GM

This story has its genesis all the way back in the year 1943 in Buffalo, New York. This was the year my life story began, setting the stage for my General Motors story. Since my father (1919–2007) was serving in the United States Army as a staff sergeant in the European Theater during World War II, I did not have him in my life full time until I was three years old. He was stateside when I was born, and when I was about ten months of age, he came home for a furlough prior to going overseas to fight the war in France.

After that visit I was attached at the hip to my mother until his return at the conclusion of the war, at which time I was about three and a half. He was a total stranger to me, and this remoteness lasted for most of my growing-up years. There was always a distance between us that—although difficult to explain—is not part of this story.

My grandparents on both my mom's and my dad's sides were legal immigrants from Poland to the United States who endured the Great Depression and the challenges of the war effort and all that went along with that. They led a modest life of thrift, which was necessary at that time and that remained with them and their generation, often called the Greatest Generation, throughout their lives.

When I visited my mom—who is ninety-two years

young—during a recent trip to the Buffalo, New York area in November of 2010, she brought out a very old certificate that she wanted to share with my wife and I. It was a Certificate of Naturalization dated June 1, 1961, that belonged to her father, my grandfather. Mom went on to tell us how proud he had been to finally be a naturalized citizen of the United States. Even more remarkable was the fact that he was seventy-six years of age at the time. His birthdate was June 26, 1885.

Buffalo was primarily an industrial region with farms outside the city. As a result, most of the workforce worked with their hands. The men worked in factories, small foundries, construction, furniture shops, auto shops, and the like. Most of the time, the mothers stayed at home to care for the home and the children.

I especially remember my early childhood and the sense of family, because I had both sets of grandparents and a large family, including my mom's seven siblings and my dad's three brothers and all the cousins. This made for great gatherings, which many scattered families of today do not experience. In most cases, we could walk to each other's homes, which is not the norm anymore. I attended a Roman Catholic elementary school run by the Felician order of Catholic nuns and walked to and from school through eighth grade and high school. We walked in rain, shine, or snow—no busing at that time, unless you could afford the fee on the public bus. We walked!

My high school years were spent at a vocational school, where I learned the trade of patternmaking, which would eventually give me an in at the General Motors Corporation Chevrolet foundry. My cousin, who happened to live next door to me, was one year ahead of me out of high school and was hired by GM before I was. I was always active in sports, lettering for three years in high school baseball, and was the vice president of the class of 1960. At that time, not many went on to advanced studies at college but immediately began to search for employment. I was one of those looking for work, even though I graduated third in my class.

As time passed, I worked a few jobs while still searching for a place to apply my trade. I finally ended up in a small shop working as an apprentice patternmaker (later called a model maker). My goal was to follow in my cousin's footsteps and get into the apprentice program at the General Motors Chevrolet foundry, which was a big deal in the sixties in Buffalo.

After a long wait, I got into the apprentice program there, and I could hardly believe it. I remember being taken on a tour of two manufacturing plants, which simply blew me away in their enormity and complexity. There was absolutely no way for me to know what a journey I would be on for the next eighteen years and how that journey would end for me and my family as well as all the employees of that plant.

The sixties was a crazy time, however I was not at all wrapped up in what was going on at the time. There was President Kennedy's assassination in 1963, President Johnson's escalation of the Vietnam War from 1963 to 1969, as well as all of the demonstrations in opposition to the war which did not end until the Paris Peace Accords in 1973. I was hired by GM in February 1964 and was married in August of that year. My wife and I moved into an apartment and began the journey of life, ultimately including the struggle to survive the General Motors Corporation and all that went with being a long-term employee of that huge, well-thought-of company. And with the Vietnam War going on, the threat of the draft , being called up by the U.S. Army, was real for young men like me.

As my apprenticeship period began, it was exciting to go to work. Learning each day from tradesmen who were from a period that seemed far in the past and having to go to night school at the local community college gave me the feeling I was doing something worthwhile and with a future.

I had no idea that I was not in the best place with this giant corporation. As my family grew with the addition of our two daughters, I gained journeyman status, bought a home, and earned a BS degree from the State University of New York at Buffalo. My goal was to do more than merely "punch a clock" forever.

One thing led to another, and I went on to temporary supervision which was the companies' way of determining whether a management candidate was a good fit for the position. In 1975 was promoted to permanent salaried supervisor position in the department had been I hired into in 1964. Just when I thought things would be better, I found out how political the management game could be. I also found out that the CYA ("cover your a——") syndrome was ubiquitous and took precedence in much of the decision making in the managing of the plant and of its resources—people included.

This is the story of my time with the General Motors Corporation at the Tonawanda Metal Casting Plant. It covers my life one year prior to me being hired, participating in a New York State–qualified apprenticeship program, working as a journeyman patternmaker, being promoted into a supervisory position in that department, being chosen by upper management to be the Quality of Work Life coordinator for our 2,500-person plant, and finally the traumatic conclusion that neither I nor any of the thousands of employees—as well as all those who would be hurt by the collateral damage—had envisioned.

Chapter 1:
THE SQUEAKY WHEEL GETS THE GREASE

My first job in the patternmaking trade was with a small "job shop", which produced patterns from mechanical drawings. Basically these businesses produced wood patterns from drawings. These were used to make sand molds for various casting facilities (foundries), where molten metal was poured into them to cast a desired part. It was a small operation with about six employees. The pay was poor. Actually, I was earning less than what I had been receiving from my unemployment benefit. But I would pick up some valuable knowledge and insight into the trade.

After six months or so at this job shop, which had no benefits to speak of and really no long-term future, I began looking for a job that would have some benefits and a bona fide apprenticeship program. I found that in the Black Rock area of Buffalo at the Pratt & Letchworth Plant in 1961. This plant produced castings primarily for the railroad industry. I began my journey as an apprentice metal patternmaker where I would be preparing and repairing tooling for the production floor.

That job was much more structured than the previous business. I was learning each and every day; the pay was much better at $2.40 per hour; and there were benefits like medical, vacation, and so on. But it was no utopia. It was a very, very old facility; some pieces of equipment were driven by an overhead pulley system. On some Monday mornings in the winter, the snow actually blew through the windows over the weekend and had to be cleared from our work areas. Needless to say, it was very cold inside that place on most winter mornings.

At this point I was a nineteen-year-old, living at home with my parents and three brothers, who were younger than I. Our home was in a nice area at the edge of what was called the West Side and was next to the corner house where two of my cousins, Ron and Carol, lived. Cousin Ron was a year older than I, and we had attended the same high school, McKinley Vocational High School, where we had been in the same trade program. He had gone on to a local community college for a two-year mechanical engineering technician program. Through this program, he had made his way into the Chevrolet Metal Casting Plant pattern shop and was in their New York State–approved apprenticeship program.

This was exactly the place I wanted to get hired into, and I talked to him regularly about the status of hiring there. So I had a good inside operative, you might say. I was ready to count the days before I would be able to give notice at my current job that I was moving on to a much better situation—one with a future. After all, General Motors Corporation had quite a lock on domestic auto sales in the United States at the time.

Finally I was given a phone number of the director of education and training in the personnel department at GM's motor plant. This was the start of getting grease to the wheels, if you will, in my quest to get hired into the company.

So, in January 1963, I began to call a person who would get quite familiar with my telephone voice. I called early in the month, every month, for twelve straight months, and the answer was always the same: Nothing open as yet. Call again next month. Finally, after twelve months of calling, during the thirteenth call in January of 1964, the director of education and training asked if I could come in for an interview. Of course my answer was affirmative, and the appointment was made.

I must say that there were times when I didn't did not believe that anything would develop from my persistence, but the squeaky wheel does get the grease. In addition to my persistence, behind the scenes a union representative had talked on my behalf to the department management about my having two and a half years of experience in the trade and about my cousin already being a great employee in the apprentice program.

On that appointment day, as I drove up to the plant and made my way into the visitors' parking lot, I was a little apprehensive. It is a huge building with a great façade, and it's right across the street from the Niagara River in Tonawanda, New York. The plant is still there today and is an important supplier of engines to many General Motors plants.

I checked in at the reception area and was given a temporary visitors badge. After a brief and somewhat uncomfortable wait, the director of education and training for the entire complex came to the lobby and welcomed me to the plant. To this day I remember the distinct background noise of machinery and the smell of machining oils as we moved through the halls leading to the education and training office in the personnel department.

This manufacturing facility was and is where all the engine components were received from outside vendors. They were then machined, assembled, tested, and then shipped to assembly plants as complete power plants for automobiles, trucks, and marine applications. The plant that I was applying to produced the castings for the cylinder case (block), cylinder heads, intake manifolds, brake drums, exhaust manifolds, and fly wheels for GM's motor plant, and the two plants were literally only feet away from each other.

It was a huge complex with the motor plant, the casting plant, Plant Four (machining and assembly of smaller items such as cylinder heads), the forge plant, and a power plant. At its highest point, there were five plants and approximately ten thousand people employed. This was heavy manufacturing at its awesome best, and I was thrilled to be on my way to being a part of it.

Once all the paperwork and aptitude and psychological tests were completed, I was taken on a tour of the motor plant on the way back to where I would work, should I be hired. It was an eye opener. The place was simply amazing. Being a young hot-rodder with a 1955 Chevrolet, I could not believe all the parts that were waiting to move onto the production lines. Cylinder blocks and cylinder heads were everywhere, as were what seemed like millions of valve springs in large container boxes, pushrods, crankshafts, and on and on. It was hard to imagine where so many engines would go, and this, mind you, was only one of several General Motors plants—not even including the Ford and Chrysler facilities.

After the brief walk through of the motor plant, we crossed a twenty-foot-wide, covered area between it and the Chevrolet Tonawanda Foundry. (It was renamed in the mid-seventies as the General Motors Tonawanda Metal Casting Plant, probably to put a more modern spin on it and to allow our castings to find their way into vehicles other than Chevrolets without being sued.)

The casting plant had its own unique smells. Only those who have experienced it would know what I'm talking about, and they would not be able to describe it either. Consider tons and tons of sand molds being made; molten iron being poured into the molds; hot, steaming green sand; cast-iron dust; and so one. It made for a unique smell and a unique environment.

However, this would not be my primary work area, as the pattern shop was separate from the manufacturing area and was on the second floor above the plant cafeteria. I can remember walking through the door with the director of education and training and entering the shop, seeing a large, busy place with much machinery and a large number of skilled trade employees.

It had work bays all along the window side of the shop, and each had up to four men working on production equipment of all kinds. Throughout the center of the work area were lathes, milling machines, plainer, shaper, drill presses, and band saws, plus the soldering area, weld shop, cutter grinder area, and tool crib.

I realize that many of these items sound like a foreign language to most, as the service economy has become the most prevalent form of employment in the United States. However, back in the sixties and seventies, manufacturing and skilled trades was an excellent means to earn a living with no college degree.

The management offices were shared by all the managers except the superintendent and the assistant superintendent. There was a back room where lockers were and where production tooling was stored. There was only one way to get the tooling down to the foundry floor, and that was on a very large elevator. Across from the shop entry door and on the other side of a small landing was the pattern design office with four draftsmen and a supervisor.

Bottom line was, if I were to be hired, this would be home for what I thought then would be a long, long time. Back in the early sixties, people—including yours truly—thought they would spend their entire working life at a General Motors plant. It wasn't uncommon back then to work thirty, thirty-five, or forty years in a large plant before retiring.

I don't recall how long the interviewing, testing, and tour of the plants took, but it was the better part of the day. It seemed to go very well, and I left the facility feeling good about my chances of being hired.

After a couple of weeks, I was notified that I had been accepted into the apprentice program with a start date of February 14, 1964. I accepted the job offer and was extremely excited about the prospect of better wages, benefits including health care, being in a New York State–qualified apprenticeship program, and getting a shot at advancement within the corporation. This was quite a life-changing event for me, and I was anxious to get started.

Chevrolet Tonawanda Foundry Employee Badge.

Chapter 2:
APPRENTICESHIP TRAINING AT GENERAL MOTORS

FEBRUARY 1964

February 14, 1964, was my first day on the job with the General Motors Corporation at the plant. Before I walk you into the plant on that first day, I should describe what its products were, how the products were made, who the customer was, and how my trade was involved in all of it.

It was a cast-iron casting plant that produced the castings for in-line, six-cylinder engine blocks; eight-cylinder blocks (cases) for passenger cars, trucks, marine, and police applications; cylinder heads, intake manifolds; exhaust manifolds; brake drums; fly wheels; and master brake cylinders.

Without turning this into a process engineering class, a brief description of what was involved is necessary. This was a "green sand foundry," which means the molds for these parts were formed in sand mixed with water and other ingredients that were delivered to the molding lines. We provided, maintained, and revised the metal production pattern—or tooled them, as it is called. When the green sand was dropped over them and compressed, it formed half of a mold. The bottom half and the top half formed the exterior surfaces of the product.

To construct the interior configuration of the casting, cores made of baked oil sand were placed in the drag mold prior to closing the mold. All the while the melting department was filing the cupola and melting the cast iron to 2,500 degrees Fahrenheit, which was then poured into the sand molds. You have to realize what all would be involved here. On line 1 alone, 250 to 300 engine blocks per hour were being "poured off." We had eight molding lines in our plant.

Once the molds cooled to a specific temperature range, they were shaken out, chipped, ground, and shot blasted. These castings were shipped to our direct customers to be machined and assembled. When these castings were sent to our primary customer, the Chevrolet motor plant next door, they were far from a finished and workable product. They would undergo serious machining and assembly before an engine was set up on the test stand, started up, and timed. This starting and testing of each engine had to be done prior to shipment to designated assembly plants and was the most expensive operation in the entire manufacturing process of engines.

I had just turned twenty-one a month prior to my first day on the job, and I was very much in awe of the whole operation, including the pattern shop where I would be continuing my apprenticeship training so I could become a journeyman patternmaker. Since I was very interested in working on cars and doing some weekend drag racing, seeing all of the patterns for engine blocks, heads, exhaust manifolds, and so on was very exciting to me.

I will explain for you the term *apprentice* and the training program involved before going forward. At that time, an apprentice in the building trades, for example, might be hired on as a helper at first and work his or her way up by gaining the confidence of a superintendent or supervisor. There was not much formality or added schooling—just time on the job until apprentices were let out on their own. The apprenticeship program I was in consisted of ten thousand hours of very specific training. That came to two thousand hours per year in a five-year program. It was quite involved and detailed, and the apprentice had a book that spelled out every aspect of training, how many hours were to be worked in specific areas. All the sections had to be signed off by your supervisor.

When I was an apprentice, it seemed like everyone was my boss, from my immediate supervisor to all the journeymen I worked with and trained under. In addition to the drafting, layout, bench work, and machine operation in the shop, I had to go to night school at the local community technical college for a two-year Tool and Die Design certificate program. The apprentices took this program because there were no programs directly related to patternmaking at that time.

The first day on the job was intimidating. The fact that my cousin had been employed there for over a year seemed to have increased everyone's curiosity about who this new guy was. The shop was very busy; it had at least 70 tradesmen on the first shift alone, and there were the second and third shifts which had 40 and 15 workers respectively . From young guys just starting out in a trade to those who had applied their trade skills literally all over the world, they all had gathered in this shop. It's interesting to look back now and realize that that was the beginning of the end of an era in manufacturing. You see we had no computer numerical control (CNC) machines and all work was done on manual machine tools which required a very skilled operator. In the production area robotics were not introduced in this plant until 1979.

As I recall, on the second or third day on the job, my supervisor asked me to go with him to the Sand Lab, which was in the manufacturing area of the plant. There was constant testing going on to make sure all the systems in the plant were running properly, so the testing of the sand systems was just one of many. Once there, we picked up a piece of tooling that made sand biscuits for doing tensile tests of core process materials. It was a "hot box," which meant the sand mix was baked as part of the process, and it was not working properly.

We disconnected it from the air and electrical sources and wheeled it up to the shop. I was told to go over the thing, clean it up, and see if I could get it to work any better. Without any coaching, I dismantled the entire piece of equipment, cleaned all the components, and basically made it look like new. We took it back to the Sand Lab, where it was hooked up. And it worked perfectly. I guessed that I'd passed my first test, as far as having prior experience was concerned. Or so I thought. But it was not that cut and dried at GM.

Here's a case to illustrate how things were done, or not done, at GM. Through the union reps, I asked the superintendent if he would consider applying my two years or four thousand hours of experience from the apprentice program of my previous employer to the ten-thousand-hour program at the Chevrolet pattern shop. After all, two years is two years, and since I was working with very little supervision and doing everything that was asked of me, I didn't think it would be a big deal.

The superintendent—"Big Joe," as he was called—was a large man, balding, and old school, and he had an all-powerful aura about him. He was probably one of the last of that generation of manager to come up from shoveling sand in a foundry in Detroit to becoming a superintendent of a large department with no formal schooling of any kind. All he said was that he would look into it. I thought at least it was not a flat out no.

To make matters worse, I received a letter from the Department of Defense inviting me to come in for a physical for the army. Being twenty-one and with the Vietnam War going on, it was not a great invite. Now the issue of having those previous hours of experience transferred to this program became a big deal, because at that time the government was issuing deferments to apprentices who had two thousand hours in a bona fide program, such as the patternmaking apprenticeship. Big Joe could not get himself to commit to an answer until finally the apprentice committee man with our union group stepped up and talked to him about the situation. Big Joe finally said he would take care of it, but he went on a weeklong vacation without finalizing anything.

There I was, with the military on my tail, with wedding plans in the early stages, doing a great job in the program, and this was happening. I can tell you that the week he was on vacation I was very upset that such a thing could go on at GM. I still believed that this was the place to be, but there I was a couple of weeks into it and being treated like that.

The next week finally came around, and the superintendent made a decision on the amount of hours he would be willing to apply to the GM program. I was shocked to hear that he was only willing to apply a thousand, which was only 25 percent of what I had accumulated in my last position. And of course it was short of the two thousand minimum hours necessary for the deferment.

Fortunately my family had a friend who worked at the local draft board, and I had the opportunity to explain my situation to her. She called me back in a couple of days and told me that I was close enough in hours that I would not be called up. If that had not taken place, my life would undoubtedly have taken a much more difficult path.

That decision meant that I would be spending four and a half years in the GM apprenticeship program and two and a half years at my previous employer for a total of seven years of training in this trade just to become a journeyman. It's also worth mentioning here that throughout my four years of vocational high school, I was in shop class for the entire afternoon, being taught the patternmaking trade from an experienced craftsman and excellent teacher.

Recently I was told by an acquaintance associated with a local university that young people today expect to be running a company in three to five years. Except in medicine, a five-year apprenticeship is incomprehensible to most of the student body of today.

Every Friday at the end of the first shift, the apprentices were charged with a lot of housekeeping, including sweeping out work bays, dumping trash containers, and wiping down machinery. Compare this to the current student expectation of being in a management positions in a few years. The times are continuing to change, and I'm not so sure it's for the better.

Shortly after beginning the apprenticeship program, I was once again enrolled into the Erie County Technical Institute in the Tool and Die Design program, because this was the closest discipline to our trade of patternmaking. It was an evening program required for GM apprentices. The courses were paid for by Chevrolet under their Tuition Reimbursement Plan. I paid up front for the classes and they repaid it upon successfully completing the course. Fair enough.

On June 23, 1966, after completing the required twenty-eight credit hours with nothing worse than a B grade, I received my diploma in the program—another successful step in becoming a journeyman in the General Motors Corporation. However, there was some unfinished business that kept nagging at me.

After high school, I was accepted into the two-year mechanical engineering associate degree program, following the path my cousin had taken a year earlier and who was doing quite well. My problem began when the mathematics instructor (the only one for my high school) for the algebra and trigonometry classes resigned just prior to my senior year, and the school could not replace him on such short notice. It was said that he left to take on a much better-paying position in industry. (Some of us still remember when there was that kind of opportunity available.)

At the time I did not think not having taken algebra and trigonometry would be a detriment in handling basic math at the community college level. However, the class was "Basic Math for Engineers," and without that year of high school algebra and trigonometry, I was doomed to failure. I lasted two semesters and earned a B+ average for courses outside of the mathematics department but failed the math. Having to leave the school was a huge letdown on many levels, including having to quit playing the infield on the college baseball team.

Not easily discouraged, in the fall of 1966 I enrolled at a local high school in their evening program for classes in tenth- and eleventh-year mathematics—the algebra and trigonometry I had missed in high school—which I took concurrently. I attended classes five nights a week in addition to working full time and having my understanding wife at home alone much of the time. I passed the regents exams with grades of 86 and 90 percent respectfully.

All of the apprentices were scheduled to work the day shift, which got underway at seven o'clock in the morning. Sometime between mid- to late 1965, after being in the program for a little over a year, I began experiencing severe problems with my stomach. If I did not have something to eat by around 9:30 in the morning, I would have a fire in the pit of my stomach that simply would not quit. It would not allow me even to think clearly. I knew deep down what was bothering me; it was the fact that I am a perfectionist in nature and do everything with that mentality.

When I presented to my immediate supervisor a better or more efficient way to accomplish a task, I would routinely get the same response: "Yes, but do it this way for now." I could sense very early on that the management was not looking to have anyone look better than they did. There was a certain pecking order in the shop and a funny breed of cat working in there, including both the hourly and the supervisory personnel. I'm sure I could write a book about the 125 coworkers who worked in the pattern department across the three shifts.

Finally I went to the doctor, and he diagnosed it as gastritis. He told me that if I did not change my mental state and learn to relax, I would be a strong candidate for a stomach ulcer. Toward the end of the appointment, he asked, "What is bothering you?" I was embarrassed to tell him that my job at the casting plant, the one I so desperately wanted, and the environment in the pattern shop were the culprits. So I simply said something like "I don't know, but I'll figure it out."

With the help of a lot of Rolaids and a much-changed attitude I was able to get over that hurdle. To be honest, I believe that having success in the classes I took did help in this healing process.

Finally, sometime in the first quarter of 1968, I was officially deemed a journeyman metal patternmaker) in the General Motors Corporation, which included a pay increase and being assigned to the second shift (3:30 p.m. to 11:30 p.m.), where I would spend most of my eighteen years.

This was sort of a letdown for me, even though it was what I had worked so hard to attain, not only while in the program but also during the twelve months of continually calling the education and training department while trying to get into the program. There I was, twenty-five years of age, and I could only wonder what I would be doing thirty years from then. I knew that this trade and this shop would not be there that long. I was not prepared to become stagnant, as were many of the people in the shop, management included, and at that point I didn't know what to do about it.

Erie County Technical Institute

Evening Program

This certifies that

James Edward Sarafin

having completed 28 credit hours in the

Tool Design

program is entitled to this

Diploma

Given at Buffalo, New York, this 23rd day of June, 1966.

James E. Shenton
President

Norine T. Whitmore
Director of Evening School

Erie County Technical Institute Tool Design Diploma.

State of New York
NELSON A. ROCKEFELLER, Governor

Department of Labor

Certificate of Completion

for

Apprenticeship Training

This is to certify that

JAMES E. SARAFIN

has served an apprenticeship of 5 years at the trade of

PATTERNMAKER (METAL)

in the employ of CHEVROLET TONAWANDA DIVISION
GENERAL MOTORS CORPORATION

under standards approved by the Industrial Commissioner
and has qualified as a Journeyman PATTERNMAKER (METAL)

Given at Albany, New York, this 26TH day of DECEMBER, 1967

James R. Egan
Administrator
Bureau of Apprentice Training
Division of Manpower

NYS Certificate of Completion of Apprenticeship Program.

General Motors Corporation

*   *   *   *   *   *

This Is to Certify That _JAMES E. SARAFIN_

has satisfactorily completed an apprenticeship
under the General Motors Standard Apprentice Plan
in all branches of the

PATTERNMAKER - METAL Trade

at

CHEVROLET TONAWANDA FOUNDRY Division of

General Motors Corporation

*   *   *   *   *   *

Certified as a Journeyman this _26TH_ day of _DECEMBER_ , 19 _67_

John J. Komack

C. B. Buckley
Personnel Director

Joseph F. Equet

Leonard A. Ward
Plant Manager

GM Certificate of Apprenticeship Completion.

Chapter 3:
IN THE GROOVE OR IN THE RUT

APRIL 1970

About two years into my chosen career, I began having thoughts of what direction I should go to protect my future. I realized that if I took no action at all, I would be doing the same stuff for as long as the factory was there. Around the spring of 1970, I had begun to talk with a lathe operator in our shop. His name was Bill, and he was working on the first shift and going to school nights to earn his master's degree in education. He eventually earned his PhD in education—all paid for by General Motors' Chevrolet Motor Division. He eventually left General Motors Corporation as well as the state of New York.

Bill kept encouraging me to go back to school to get a degree because, as he said, Chevrolet might not be the career of my entire working life. At the time I didn't realize how prophetic that was. He and I and many other guys had a feeling of disenchantment because of the nature of most of the work in the pattern shop. The feeling of a lack of accomplishment, other than job assignment completion, and the feeling of being lost in a very small corner of a corporate giant while so much activity was going on each and every day was disconcerting.

Bill would never be considered for supervision or management because of his so-called "bad attitude." In reality, I felt that the problem was that he was outspoken and often critical of the supervisory team, even though he did this in a very informed and educated manner. I believe that the real issue was that they did not feel comfortable with a good machine operator who had also earned his BS degree and was well on his way to his master's and then his PhD. This was simply another example of General Motors paying for an employee's education while not giving him the opportunity to better himself within the corporation. How foolish.

Management's criticism of this employee revealed an interesting undercurrent of envy and dislike of an educated subordinate. The management team at that point had a department head whom I will call Joe. To the best of anyone's knowledge, Joe did not have a high school diploma. He had come up the organization the hard way, although not necessarily a bad way, shoveling sand in a foundry in Detroit. His journey from that point to his current position as a department head in GM was unknown to us.

The assistant department head, Larry, who had a high school diploma, was very sharp when it came to the reading of engineering drawings and understanding pattern design, as well as other nuances of the shop. He made his boss look good time and again, and this was the primary reason he went from draftsman to pattern shop supervisor to general supervisor and finally to assistant department head in an extremely short time.

At that time, all of the first-line supervisors, except Mac, had high school diplomas. Even so, he enjoyed the position of general supervisor and would, without a doubt, be moving up to assistant department head as soon as the current occupant retired. He was a real politician and pushed his agenda always. He was all I, I, me, me.

Bill, my lathe operator friend, would never be offered an opportunity for supervision, or management in general, because the powers that be in the shop were quite uncomfortable with him. They knew full well they could not snow him, and I felt that they must have felt disarmed to come to the point of accusing him of having a bad attitude. This was scary to me because I felt that this could happen to anyone who tried to better themselves, including me. As my story unfolds, I found out this fear was well founded.

The three shifts in our department were filled with 125 skilled tradesmen who came from all over the country and hung their shingle at the casting plant. Without a doubt, without the work we did on the pattern tooling, the plant would have had zero success in producing a viable product.

With that said, I can tell you that we also stretched the rules when it came to some of our behavior, and I would like to tell you of just a few of those times. Because I worked most of my years at GM on the second shift, I am more familiar with and can accurately comment on some of the stuff that went on during that shift. I believe some of what went on was really a response to being in a rut and needing a little diversion.

On the day shift and working in the first bay, where he could be easily seen, was Gary the magician. No lie. This guy did gigs all over the Buffalo area, and he practiced his card tricks right at his bench for hours during working hours. I guess you could call him a magician to be able to get away with it; he got away with it because supervision did not want to deal with him. When management came rushing down the aisle with a "hot" rush job, the magician would put the cards away and make like he was hard at work. And they would always walk right by him and give the assignment to someone who was working steadily on a project during the whole shift.

One of my shop friends was Jerry, and if you saw him then, you would know right away that he was a body builder. One day we decided that since we had more than the legal thirty minutes for lunch, we would do weight training in our locker area adjacent to the shop. We proceeded to cut steel bar for the barbell and dumbbells, grabbed various castings, such as fly wheels, from the scrap bins as weights, and made our own locking collars. We even had a chinning bar that went from one metal tooling rack to another. A short time after beginning our workouts, I began to bulk up and then had to cut back a bit because I felt it would affect my golf game.

To celebrate on the eve of holidays, such as Thanksgiving, Christmas, or the Fourth of July, we would arrange to bring in food—and lots of it. On one occasion, in addition to the snacks that folks brought, we ordered a six-foot submarine sandwich that was delivered to the plant on a long wooden board. The plant security guards thought it was a hoot and so did all the employees as we passed them on the way to our department. A great meal was had by all, supervisors included, and I can tell you the last three hours of the shift were tough to get through. Really, a nap would have been in order.

On another occasion we decided to bring in Polish sausage and sauerkraut, mustard, pickles, great buns, and crock pots to heat everything. Naturally we had to begin the heating process prior to our lunch period, and as the Polish sausage and kraut began to warm, the aroma of it permeated the entire department. We could only hope that no big brass would visit our department on a business matter, and none did that evening.

Finally, to satisfy some of our competitive juices, we had rubber horseshoes, and we played with them in one of the large aisles. Of course, most games were played for small stakes. It was obvious that we were in the groove as well as in a rut.

Chapter 4:
DECISION TIME—BACK TO SCHOOL

Because of the many discussions with my friend Bill, as well as my desire to improve, I decided to enroll in a biology class at the State University of New York in Buffalo. I felt I had to do it right then, even though it was the summer semester, 1970. I was fearful that if I delayed, chances were that I may not begin at all.

The summers in Buffalo are extremely short, and because I was an avid golfer, this was really hard for me to do. I had one class in the morning and then was off to work by 2:45 in the afternoon for the second shift. Well, I got through the course with a B grade, played some golf, and was extremely happy that I had my four-year college degree program underway.

Buffalo State, as it was called at that time, was primarily a teaching college, but they were adding programs to expand the appeal of the institution. Because I wasn't interested in teaching or engineering, I enrolled in the criminal justice degree program. The department recruiters told me about the many avenues I could take after graduation with a BS degree. One was to use the degree to enable my advancement within General Motors; law enforcement was always in play, such as being a probation or parole officer; and last but not least was law school, which was a choice of several of the graduates.

The curriculum was general in scope, cutting through almost all disciplines, as most college electives do. I also had the opportunity to produce actual pretrial sentencing reports, which were used by the judges to assist them in determining the penalty to be meted out to the convicted person. To provide them, I was required to interview the defendant in jail, and I also went into the community to interview neighbors and relatives to gather the information the judge required in order to administer a proper sentence. This was an experience I have never forgotten, and I believe it helped me all through my life in working with people of all personalities.

I would be receiving my degree in May of 1974, and I was feeling better and better about what I was about to accomplish. But it was a tough row to hoe. I was married all the while, had two great little daughters, and worked full time on the second shift, including many Saturdays. One of the things I was and am most proud of was the fact that I took full-time credit hours for my last two semesters. With all that was on my plate, I still managed to earn a 3.43 GPA.

Prior to my final semester, an incident took place involving me and our new department head that shocked me, especially in light of the major goal I would soon be reaching. I took my school voucher form, which was required by the Tuition Refund Program, to be signed by the department head. As I handed the forms to him, I said, "Well, this will be the last time you will have to sign one of these."

He replied, "Why is that?" I told him that upon completing that semester, I would be graduating with a Bachelor of Science degree. He paused a moment and replied, "I don't know whether to offer you my congratulations or my condolences."

I almost fell over in disbelief. The last thing I expected was a putdown after all the hard work I had put into it and with a final semester to go. I did not have a reply, because I was totally unprepared to hear something like that and because I didn't have the experience to enable me to respond without cutting my own throat. After all, his comment was totally unprofessional, and I probably should have told him so in no uncertain terms. I believe that what he was alluding to was the fact that even though I had put so much into my college education, the department's management team at the time did not want me to come on board, regardless of my ability and soon-to-be college degree. This is my opinion, of course.

As anticipated, I graduated with a BS in criminal justice on May 26, 1974. As I recall, this came and went without much fanfare. Congratulations came mostly from my wife, some family members, and a few of my closer friends at the casting shop. Then it was back to the grind, and I would have to determine how or if I would or could use the degree to open up my options for me.

STATE UNIVERSITY OF NEW YORK

COLLEGE AT BUFFALO

ON THE RECOMMENDATION OF THE FACULTY
AND BY VIRTUE OF THE AUTHORITY VESTED IN THEM
THE TRUSTEES OF THE UNIVERSITY HAVE CONFERRED ON

JAMES EDWARD SARAFIN

THE DEGREE OF

BACHELOR OF SCIENCE

AND HAVE GRANTED THIS DIPLOMA AS EVIDENCE THEREOF
GIVEN IN THE CITY OF BUFFALO IN THE STATE OF NEW YORK
IN THE UNITED STATES OF AMERICA ON THE TWENTY-SIXTH DAY
OF MAY ONE THOUSAND NINE HUNDRED AND SEVENTY-FOUR

Chairman of the Board of Trustees

Chairman of the College Council

Chancellor of the State University of New York

President of the College

*Diploma from the State University of
New York College at Buffalo.*

I was thirty-one at the time, and I decided that law school would not be a fit for me. I did make an attempt to have an interview with the New York State Police, but their response to me by letter was that I was "too old to be a candidate." This kind of thing would not happen now, but back in 1974 it did. In retrospect, I should have fought to get into the training academy. I also went to Florida and interviewed with the State Probation and Parole Department. That went so well that it could have been an immediate hire. However, I did have a family to consider; I would have had to take a 50 percent cut in pay. I respectfully declined and continued to punch the clock while contemplating my future.

UNEXPECTED HELP ARRIVES

Since I already had ten years of service at General Motors, I decided that I should give management a shot and try to get an opportunity as a temporary supervisor. In that position I would maintain my union status while covering the department when supervisors were out because of illness, vacation, and so on.

Two representatives of the Pattermakers League of North America, which I was a member, began to go to management on my behalf, explaining to them that I should get a shot at temporary supervision the next time an opening came about. That was a great perk of being a union member, and it was very nice of them to do that for a coworker. One of these men also went downstairs to push the agenda to the personnel director. Fortunately, things began to happen.

In July of 1976, twenty-six months after my graduation from college, I was summoned to the shop office to talk with Bill Mac, the general supervisor of the second shift. He asked me to have a seat. And right off the bat and very bluntly he asked me if I would be interested in temporary supervision. I didn't have to think about the answer, because this had been one of my goals since I had gone back to school. I told him, "Yes, thank you, I would love to give it a shot."

And so the journey at GM continued, and for the first time I had a chance at upward mobility. I could never have imagined what the next five years would be like—some of it very good and some of it simply awful.

Chapter 5:
THE LONG ROAD TO MANAGEMENT

In July of 1976 I accepted the offer for a temporary supervisor position in our model shop. But unbelievably, my general supervisor, Mac, spent much of the orientation meeting telling me how he had fought to convince the management group that I would do well in supervision. He felt the skills of the trade I had, the knowledge of the production tooling, and the college degree made me a good fit for the position.

Right then and there I believed he was full of it and that if he had it his way, I would not get a sniff of advancement, period. What I do believe is that it was time for the plant and our department to begin looking at employees with college degrees—people who demonstrated that they were serious about advancing their careers in General Motors. I also believe that this education thing was really upsetting the status quo in the shop. They wanted to remain in the "do it my way" method of management, whereby no one could get any credit for ideas but the anointed ones.

As you may recall, my General Motors story began in January of 1963. I was called in for an initial interview and testing in January of 1964 and was hired in February of 1964. I earned journeyman patternmaker (model maker) status in 1968 and graduated from Buffalo State in May of 1974. Finally, in July of 1976, I was asked if I had an interest in giving management a shot.

I'm sure your math skills are good enough for you to figure

out that it took me over thirteen years from the time I began at the casting plant to being queried by my boss as to my intentions regarding my interest in supervision. I hope the kids in college now, who expect to run a company in three years, get to read my story so they can have just a little more patience in pursuing their careers.

Another hourly employee, Joe, was looking toward supervision in the pattern service group (the folks who changed all the production tooling to accommodate the production schedules). He and I were the first two employees in the casting plant to be involved in a new corporate eight-week training program for those entering temporary supervision. This also put us on the first shift to attend the classes and do the workbook assignments along with shadowing a current supervisor. And, as usual, the shift change to days caused angst. We were under the advisement of a real nice man in the personnel department who later took a leave of absence from the plant to attend the University of Michigan in pursuit of a PhD. When he received his PhD, he never returned to GM.

I saw many young men, educated at the General Motors Institute in Flint, Michigan, leave the company once they realized their future would not be as promising as they had thought. The corporation was spending good money to educate them and then did not know what to do with them. It was a shame, really.

The plant was very busy during this time, and we were working twelve days on and one day off. It was a New York State law that you were not allowed to work thirteen days straight. This was going on for quite a while and no doubt was a contributing factor in our assistant department head having a heart attack at the plant. Fortunately it was not a terribly serious attack, but he was gone for some time to recover.

At about the same time, around the end of July or early September of 1976, the most junior supervisor suffered a broken foot when it was run over by a lift truck. Because of these two incidents, the shop was suddenly down to two management people. Things began to get interesting as far as scheduling both regular and temporary supervision.

Because of this, Joe and I were pressed into action before completing the new training program for temporary supervisors. We filled the two openings created by the medical issues. More importantly, we were not shadowing veteran supervisors, as was supposed to be the case, but working alone. This did not surprise me at all, as things were always changing to suit their needs—even if it was not the right thing to do. After all, at that point, we were not even classified as temporary supervisors.

The days went by, and even though we were doing our thing on the shop floor, we completed the eight-week program of interviews and written material in four weeks. During one conversation, my department head, Dan Q, told me, "Your education shows by what you've done in the workbook." The superintendent of manufacturing, Ken G, took my workbook and used it as an example of how trainees should approach the project. That was cool.

In October of 1976 I made temporary supervision status, but I didn't even know about it. I came in for the first shift on Monday morning, expecting to be told to go back to my position on the shop floor but the decision had been made to keep me in the temporary supervisory position. I had completed another step on the road to making the management team at GM.

The process of me going from temporary to permanent supervision was amazing , especially when you think of General Motors as one of the greatest corporations of all time. The reason I say this is that the process was, in my opinion, unprofessional, shoddy, and incomplete. Temporary supervisors could be kept on the floor for fifteen weeks after which they were to go back to their hourly positions. Since my fifteen weeks would be over two days after the Christmas holiday, which was almost two weeks long, I felt that pattern shop management should have made their decision and notified me prior to the holiday break, however that did not happen. That was the GM way as I experienced it.

Around the last week of November or the first week of December of 1976, Bill B., the assistant master mechanic, called me into the office and very informally asked if I was interested in taking the job. Now, mind you, after all the degree work, pushing to get the door opened, going through the temp program, he was still asking me if I was "interested." I suppose he wanted to get my thoughts prior to going public and processing the required paperwork, since the last person to take the job lasted only two weeks before going back to hourly. I believe the management group had been in a state of shock because that particular employee was the person they preferred, and for him to reverse course like that was very problematic.

As unbelievable as this may seem, I have to tell you that at no time during that meeting was there any discussion of salary or benefits. I was simply asked if I was interested in the job and responded by saying if I was not interested, I would not have stayed on through the entire process. After thanking him his response was, "Okay, the paperwork will be put in".

Like it or not, they were now committed and would not be able to put me on the backburner any longer. Like it or not, they were going to have me on their team. And in those days, the new General Motors slogan in the plants was "The #1 Team."

Chapter 6:
EMPLOYEE/MANAGEMENT RELATIONS IN THE TRENCHES OF A CORPORATE GIANT

On December 1, 1976, I officially began my salaried management career on the second shift. I was to begin receiving the final required management training so that I could be on my own in the shop. It was exciting as well as a little unsettling. There I was, being prepared to supervise the very skilled tradesmen whom I had worked alongside and who had showed me the nuances of the trade during my four years of apprenticeship. I felt ready to take on the responsibility, and I truly believed that I could make a difference.

To this day, I will never forget how excited I was on December 15, 1976, when I received my first salaried paycheck. However, I had actually taken a sixteen-dollar cut for the month. That was upsetting, to say the least, and difficult to fathom. I thought there had been a bookkeeping error. As soon as I had the chance, I went downstairs to the personnel department to sign all the required paperwork. That's when I was hit with the actual compensation figure. I almost fell through the floor, and to this day I do not know what kept me there to complete all the forms. My thought at the time was, *this must be the GM way.* Upper management, the board of directors, the stockholders, and the purchasers of GM products had and probably still have no idea this kind of thing went on in General Motors.

As soon as I returned to the shop, I stopped to discuss this with my department head. I explained to him that when I agreed to accept the promotion into salaried supervision, I did not envision having to take a pay cut. Wouldn't it be realistic to expect an increase in pay for the increase in responsibilities? He told me he would make an adjustment to my compensation after the holiday *and* after the contract negotiations in the plant. (The United Auto Workers [UAW] union was in the final stages of its contract negotiations. The salaried workforce as well as the Patternmakers League of North America, which I was a member of, could expect a wage increase commensurate with that which the hourly workforce achieved.) I said, "Thank you." What else could I have done about it? Quit? No way.

The days and weeks went by swiftly, helped along by the fact that the plant would be shut down prior to the Christmas holiday and would not be back in operation until a day after New Year's Day. The plant did not always shut down during this period, but because of the disruption and absenteeism that usually occurred, the managers of the four plants in the complex felt that it made more sense to shut everything down. That turned out to be a paid holiday.

THE YEAR IS 1977

If you took a look back at the year 1977, you would see that this was the year when the wheels really began to fall off this great corporation, General Motors, and in particular in my plant, which had made plenty of money for Chevrolet and the General Motors Corporation over the previous two-plus decades.

On March 1, 1977, almost two months after I was promoted to a permanent, salaried, sixth-level supervisor position, my paycheck was mercifully correct for the first time. In my first two months, the following errors were present, even though I signed a plethora of forms in the process: My name was spelled "Serafin" rather than "Sarafin." The last two digits of my Social

Security number were interchanged. Payroll had not deducted the premium for the comprehensive medical plan for my family and me. There also was no purchase of GM stock deducted. And, finally, no deduction was made for the United Way Fund, which I had signed up for and which all salaried people were highly encouraged to participate in. All of this took place even though all the forms I had handed in were 100 percent correct. I had the copies.

This was about the time in my General Motors career when I began to wonder how in the world it was possible for a casting to be produced, an assembled engine to come out of the motor plant, or a complete vehicle to be driven out of an assembly plant when they couldn't even get an employees' data correct.

On March 3, 1977, I asked the department head about the pay adjustment he told me he would take care of after the Christmas holiday. Mind you, this was sixty days since coming back from the holiday. He showed me a handful of forms and told me he was in the process of raising all the supervisors' salaries in our department. This was going to take approximately another month. Well, this pay issue was finally resolved, but I really do not recall if the adjustment was ever rectified at that time. I just had to go with the flow at GM and keep on doing my best. What else could I do?

At the end of March, the twenty-eighth to be exact, Ken , the superintendent of manufacturing for the second shift, called our office and asked me, yes me, if I was going to the American Foundry Society annual dinner and dance in early April. I did not even know of the event and had no idea why he asked me if I was going. Maybe he had come to like me while I was in the supervisor training program. But I never found out.

When I informed my supervisor, Mac, of this, I could see he wasn't thrilled. After all, I was new on the team, so why would a manufacturing superintendent ask me to attend such an event? It would also mean that he would have to stay the entire evening on that Saturday, unlike all the other Saturdays, when he skipped out early and left me alone in the shop until eleven. I called my wife to let her know of the event, and later that evening I mentioned to Bill that I was interested in going. He merely said okay.

Things went south from this point forward. I came into the office the next day and sat down with my two supervisors, who were talking about the usual shop stuff. Almost as if it were an afterthought, big Bill said to me, "Oh, by the way, you're starting day shift Monday." Now, mind you, it was already Tuesday, so I wondered when I would have been told if I hadn't walked into the office right then. He also asked me how long I thought it would take me to be comfortable running the tool changing group, called Pattern Service, on my own. I told him no longer than a couple of weeks, because I had already run the shop on my own on several occasions. Actually, I could have taken over immediately, but I did not want it to look as if I were cocky or any such thing as that.

It was around 10 p.m. this day when I asked Mac, "What should I tell my wife about Saturday night?" He told me to let Ken know that I could attend and I could pick up the tickets at the shop on Saturday. I thanked him, left a message with the superintendents' secretary at eleven, and left for the day. You see, he wanted me to come in on Saturday, as we had been doing for some time, to work for two or three hours and then to rush around to get to the event. I knew that if I worked for only two hours that day, I would be done at 5:30 and have to rush to the event at seven.

He could have very easily told me not to come in on that Saturday, and he could have had the tickets for me the day before. But that was not the way things were done. I thought it was pretty crappy when this is the guy who had tried to convince me that he had talked his two superiors into putting me on as supervisor. Life goes on, and you just go with the flow.

Well, as luck would have it, I went in to the plant on Wednesday and Mac told me that Ken, the manufacturing superintendent, had my tickets for the dinner. An hour into the shift he came up to the shop and gave them to me and I could sense that Bill did not like how that had gone down. Now the question would come up about why I should even come in on that Saturday because I already had the tickets. As it turned out that question never came up because on the Thursday prior to the event, we found out that our Pattern Service supervisor, who hurt his knee the day before, was having knee surgery that Friday. I'm sure you can figure out what happened next. No dinner and no Saturday off. It would be the twelfth Saturday in succession that I worked in the shop. In the end, there were only three of eight production molding lines running, and I was basically done with everything in the first hour. I could have easily gone to the dinner, but that is how things happened in the trenches of the casting plant.

In the summer of 1977, on June 28, I finally had my vacation for the first week of August approved. It was like pulling teeth, as I had to push and push to get them to make this "huge" decision. When I consider all the consecutive days I'd worked, including Saturdays and Sundays, the long hours and double shifts through snowstorms, I found it to be gross mismanagement by upper management to be so reluctant to make a decision for a one-week vacation. In their eyes, one minute you were messing up, and the next, they couldn't do without you.

RECORD PROFIT VS. TAILSPIN

On July 31, 1977, General Motors Corporation posted a net profit of 1.1 billion dollars for the second quarter. That was a new record, but it would be the last record earnings period that I would experience while an employee at GM.

Though this was great news for the company, it wasn't so great for one of my brothers, who worked as a toolmaker apprentice in the motor plant. I was able to lay the groundwork that opened the door for him to get into the program, and he would have been a great asset for GM. However, not only he but all of the newly hired motor plant toolmaker apprentices were given layoff notices, even though there was all kinds of work to do in the plant. My brother told me he'd heard that the plant manager had failed to appropriate the funds for the apprentice program, so they all had to go. I found it incomprehensible that with the announcement of a record quarter for the corporation, they pushed apprentices out the door.

ONLY AT CHEVY

On August 10, 1977, I was on the day shift—or first shift, as it was called—as the supervisor of pattern service group. If you remember, these were the guys whose primary job was to mount production tooling onto the molding machines and core-making machines. Very simply, a mold generally creates the exterior of a product, and one or many cores form the inner surface and contours. As an example, both an engine block and a cylinder head have water jackets, created by cores, to keep the engine from overheating. They are internal and are seen only when the engine is disassembled.

The day began with three men absent out of a group of ten. That itself created a problem, because these guys did hard and dangerous work. Being 30 percent short on manpower was no small matter.

At about 7:30 a.m., I received word that the core room superintendent was asking to have a certain production machine's tooling changed. I went down to the production area and by eight had my people lined up to make the complete change. I also had to get the pipefitters and electricians involved to do their thing. The pipefitters didn't show up until thirty to forty-five minutes later. And because our only stacker truck with a lift was in the garage for repair, I had to scrounge one from the maintenance department. All the tooling had to be found, pulled out of where it was, and delivered to the production machine. During all of this running around and waiting for other departments to respond, our team had the machine totally stripped by 9:30 a.m., which was remarkable.

At this point my crew went on their fifteen minute contractual break, and I went upstairs to the pattern shop to let them know how things were going and to get my own break in. That's when it got interesting. As soon as I arrived in our office, Bill Mac, told me that the core room superintendent had called and was wondering what the holdup was on the machine. I had been away from the scene for about ten minutes, and he was making an ass of himself calling up to our department. Immediately after that the assistant plant manager called our department head with the same concern.

Keep in mind that neither of these men was calling around when we were waiting for help from the other departments and that my guys had contractual breaks that had to be honored. At that point I get called in to the big man's office to explain what was going on. After hearing my assessment of the goings on, he told me that "when Joe W [the production superintendent] gets it stuck up his ___, somebody pays."

We were able to complete the entire changeover in three hours, at eleven, which was an hour and a half less than what our Industrial Engineering Department Standards had listed. I thanked my crew, but I didn't get a thank-you from my supervisors. And amazingly, at 3:00 p.m., at the end of my day, I was told that the machine was still not making any product (cores). Only at Chevy!

On August 19, 1977, I made my first entry in my diary for a while, not because there had been a lack of material but because I was always exhausted at the end of the workday. With that said, I will attempt to condense the maddening situation in the plant.

The plant had been running very poorly and July had the poorest production numbers in a very long time. This was brought on by equipment issues and high scrap rates due in part to the many production tooling changes that had become the norm. Scrap rates were determined by taking the number of castings produced that were rejected by inspection divided by the total number produced. Items the inspectors would be looking for included metal hardness, cracked castings, missing identification numbers, and porous metal to name a few. Many issues were contributing to this poor performance and August was continuing on the same course as July. It was disturbing, to say the least.

The plant manager had been spending considerable time on the production floor, which was unusual. All of a sudden, the stuff hit the fan, and he completely lost his cool. We all thought that his boss in Saginaw, Michigan, was putting pressure on him to produce more and more castings each day, so he was roaming the plant and literally terrorizing everyone from superintendents to hourly workers. He verbally violently attacked my people for sitting in their staging area, though they had always done that when they were waiting for the next tooling change or quick repair that did not require a skilled trade. I attempted to explain that to him, but he would not hear it. Then I explained what had gone down to the production superintendent, but he was in no position to change the plant manager's take on the matter.

To make things worse, the plant manager went to my department head's office and told him he did not want to see more than two people in their designated area. This designated area is where the phone was located for us to contact them. I had men scattered everywhere, and not knowing where they were would make it that much more inefficient to get tooling changes done. My boss was powerless to refute this decision, and so life went on—but with more difficulty.

All of the chairs and benches had to be thrown out, because guys who were working eleven hours a day and six days a week could not sit down between assignments. Ridiculous! Situations like that did nothing to improve plant performance and surely had a negative effect on morale. In my diary I wrote the following: "This is inhumane and disgraceful and I feel ashamed to be a part of it."

The following day, I got another slap in the face during lunchtime. I noticed a memo on the desk from the department head to the assistant department head outlining tentative subjects for our upcoming Monday management meeting. The subjects included the usual items, such as housekeeping, newspapers, early quits, and vacations. But his list of supervisor assignments had me slated for the second shift. Blood shot out of my eyes. Under normal circumstances this would have been fine, except I was to begin attending night classes on the first of September for an MBA program at the Canisius College.

Prior to pursuing an MBA, I had received the blessing of my department head, who also wrote a letter of recommendation to the school for me. He also told me to work out the schedule with the two Bills. Well, there I was, at the twelfth hour, having already paid my 525-dollar deposit. I made up my mind then and there that I would be attending school, even if it meant leaving supervision and going to the day shift, back to working my trade as a union employee.

On the following Monday, I sat down with the assistant department head who, quite astonishingly, told me, "We can't let school stand in the way of running the department efficiently." Well, I almost fell over, and of course nothing was resolved at that time. A couple more days passed, and I still had heard nothing from the powers that be.

Fast-forward to September 22. I'd been taking classes for

three weeks already. A meeting was in process in the office of our department head, including the assistant department head and my immediate boss. It went on for three-quarters of an hour. When they emerged, I was told by the assistant department head, "You start third Monday."

Now, keep in mind that they all knew about my request to further my education, but they had procrastinated and then tried to snow me, which would cost me money and the opportunity to get an MBA, all under the guise that we had a supervisor rotation problem. The fact was that there were only two supervisors out of the entire management group who rotated: me and my whining counterpart, who was very tight with my immediate boss.

This was not a shift that I could work for a long period, and I assumed that I would be able to rotate between it and the day shift. But that was tough. Imagine for a minute going into the plant at 10:30 in the evening, leaving at 7:30 in the morning, arriving home at eight, and then trying to get some sleep until mid-afternoon. For me, late afternoon and early evening was either study time or off to evening classes. Keep in mind; I was married with two daughters. It was a difficult situation.

During these times, there was always something going on in the plant. It was about the first week of October of 1977 when we were informed that we were having a change in plant managers. Now a change in plant managers is no small item, however it was understandable given how poorly the plant had been operating. Eventhough he served GM well for many years he, sometimes referred to as the wild German, was shipped out to exile to an old Detroit forging plant. In his place marched in a career Marine with crew cut and all. Less than two weeks into his tenure I was told that he was tape recording all of his staff meetings. In my view, if his object was to find out what was going on, as the new plant manager, he would want everyone speaking freely. It all seemed very strange to me.

The next little incident was typical of many other incidents throughout my supervisory years in that shop. Mac, my general supervisor, showed me a large, eight-cylinder case pattern that we had to continue working on during my third shift. As soon as he told me what they were doing and why, I made a suggestion for an alternative way to proceed, because that tactic did not look like it would correct the problem. He gave me some of his BS and said it would be fine to do it his way. I assigned the project to a couple of my guys and told them to work on all of the other areas but that one. I said we would discuss it further when the first shift came in.

At about 7:10 a.m., I talked to the new general supervisor, and he also rejected my idea. I believe that Bill got to him before I did. I was walking out of the shop when one of the layout men called out to me. He told me that "they" had decided to revise the pattern as I had been suggesting. I thought, *What?!* Someone other than me had made the suggestion, and it was accepted. For some silly reason, they tried their best to keep my name out of the picture. I wondered how we would be able to compete with the Japanese auto companies with attitudes like that.

At the end of November 1977, we were having a seventy-thousand-dollar piece of machinery set up in our shop. Though it was new to us, it was an Italian-made six-head, or station, duplicator that had to be twenty years old. The various machining heads were all shimmed because of all the wear and tear on the key areas of the unit. The six heads would never be used simultaneously because our pattern equipment was simply too large. It was an old machine really meant for smaller projects than what we had. There we were, closing in on the year 1978, and a department in the General Motors Corporation had purchased a piece of crap. These kinds of situations made me wonder how much longer GM, and in particular that individual plant, could continue in the ever-changing and challenging world of manufacturing.

1978 BEGINS WITH A BANG

The long Christmas holiday was over, and we all returned to work on Tuesday, January 3. A message was posted about a management meeting in our department that all supervisors were required to attend. The meeting was scheduled for the next day from two to three in the afternoon. As I was on the third shift, having to come in at two in the afternoon for a meeting was no fun, believe me. Thankfully the shop ran as smoothly as you could expect for the first day back from a long holiday, which was very welcome.

The meeting was different from all other meetings in our department. First, the department head took the lead, saying, "Gentlemen, we have lost control." He said that, even though we had done a good job in the past, "you must now do better, or I will get people who can." He went on to tell us that if he went out into the shop and witnessed bad behavior, he would discipline the employee himself and he would also reprimand his supervisor. I suppose all that "chain of command" stuff didn't apply to him. His rationale for this was that the plant was running at 68 percent efficiency when 80 percent or higher was the goal.

Immediately after the meeting, I approached the assistant department head and suggested that it may be time to put the third-shift lunch period back to thirty minutes, as the contract read. After all, I said, what would happen to me as the supervisor letting this go on while the plant was going in a downhill spiral? I told him it would likely cause quite the uproar and would be met with much resistance, since it had gone on for at least the last fifteen years. He listened and gave me the green light.

As I was driving home after the meeting, I could not get the situation out of my mind. These were all high-seniority men on this shift, and they had done the job for many years of keeping the production departments happy during the evening and early-morning hours. However, not much else was done in between. I knew that addressing the amount of non-productive time on this shift, as well as a couple of other items, would cause a very bitter response. However, by doing nothing, I would be tagged as the supervisor who let his men have double the time for lunch, did not enforce safety regulations at all times, and allowed newspapers to be spread out on workbenches during work hours. No great choice here.

Early in the shift the following day, I asked the third-shift union committeeman to come into the office. I explained to him the content of the management meeting that had taken place earlier in the day and about the backlash coming, due to the plant running so poorly. Additionally I told him that the department head had laid out what he expected from his supervisors and of the employees on the floor.

The following was the content of the new rules, none of which should have been a big deal: No newspapers or magazines in the work area other than at break time and during lunch. Adhere to wearing safety glasses and side shields as required, and adhere to the thirty-minute lunch period. They also had two ten-minute breaks.

Well, he was visibly upset and told me that I would have to be the one to tell the men, which I proceeded to do in a diplomatic way to four and five at a time in the supervisors' office. It was two and a half hours of difficult discussion, because as simple as the request was, they were being asked to give up the way *they* wanted the shop to run and the way management had allowed things to work.

Later in the shift, the men held an impromptu meeting where *they* decided to continue their sixty-minute lunch break in direct defiance of my requests. When I told the union committeeman I did not believe the decision was a wise one, he said, "Why don't you keep the one-hour lunch and tell your general supervisor, or anyone else for that matter, that the thirty-minute lunch is in effect." He went on to say that if anyone came up to the shop during that time that I could hit the buzzer, and the workers would get up from a nap or put away the newspapers. How could they respond when they were asleep? This was a ridiculous.

I had to remind him that I would not be the only supervisor on their shift. What would happen when the next supervisor found out that the revised lunch period was a hoax? After all was said and done the workers made their beds, shut off the lights, and took an hour nap. It was business as usual for them with zero regard for me or the contractual agreement. I was floored.

After the end of the shift, I went to the Labor Relations Office, because I now knew that this was not going to be easy; I needed some guidance and support. A subsequent meeting with my immediate supervisor and our department head put the wheels in motion. When I arrived for work the following day, a notice by the department head was on the bulletin board at the clock-in station. It clearly stated what was required of the third shift in regard to lunchtime. Everything went smoothly that evening, but there was an undercurrent of discontent throughout the entire department as well as all the shifts.

VALENTINE'S DAY 1978

One wonders why there were attitudes within the General Motors Corporation and the casting plant that were extremely detrimental to their profitability. I believe this next story sums it up well.

A very close female acquaintance of mine was laid off on Valentine's Day in 1978 from the Harrison Radiator plant in Lockport, New York. You might ask why this event had any significance. It's not like she was the only person ever laid off from GM. But the circumstances make this the story that it is.

I had been instrumental in assisting her in gaining employment at the Chevrolet casting plant, which was making a conscious effort to hire some female employees. The plant was only a fifteen-minute drive for her, and even though she knew the foundry environment was tough, she really wanted to be able to earn a good salary along with benefits. She was hired in May of 1978 and was excited as well as anxious about it.

Her position was on a molding line as a heavy core setter, where she placed various sand cores into a large fixture, locked it up, and set them in each mold as they went by. She was a very good and conscientious employee, not one of those employees constantly on the absentee roles or running to Medical during their shift for a headache simply to get out of work.

In mid-January of 1979, she was laid off because molding line 1, which she was assigned to, was being shut down for modernization. She didn't mind it at the time, because she welcomed the opportunity to rest a little from the grind of five- and six-day weeks doing a repetitive task in a rough environment. Spending a little quality time with her three daughters was also welcomed.

After five weeks of being laid off, she received an unsolicited call from the GM Harrison Radiator plant personnel department, asking her if she would be willing to go to work there. This was unexplainable to her and to me, because she had not signed up for the UAW's "area hire list" and therefore should not have been contacted about the open position. However, since she was contacted, she had to accept the offer, even though the plant was over thirty miles from her home. She went to the plant the following Monday, took a physical, and was back the next day for an all-day orientation, after which she was told to report for work the following Monday.

She reported for her shift that first day and was put on the job. She told me that almost immediately the production line employees told her that they could not understand why she and the others from the casting plant were hired into their plant.

They explained that they had seniority workers currently laid off from the plant, so why hire people from other plants? This was disconcerting to her, and she called and asked me about it. I told her that I didn't have an answer and that she had to hang in there and see what developed.

When she reported for work on the Friday of the first week of employment, her supervisor informed her that it would be her last day. She was flabbergasted, in disbelief, and now would have to reapply for unemployment insurance and go through another two-week waiting period for the one week of work she had put in at that plant. For what purpose?!

Even though I was not totally surprised by this, I was still amazed that the General Motors Corporation and one of its plants could screw up on a rather simple procedure such as that. The consequence of this blunder was turmoil for an employee, because what they did made no sense whatsoever. The question in my mind, as well as hers, was whether she would be called back to the casting plant once the updated molding line 1 was put back into production. Well, because of declining orders and weak sales, she was never called back to work there, effectively ending her GM career at five months and one week.

One explanation for this situation was that, prior to this, the casting plant had but a few women in the building. They were in personnel, were department manager secretaries, and were nurses in the medical department. The manufacturing floor was primarily male. The corporation must have wanted to push for some sort of balance in the plants and so had issued a directive to all plant managers that they should hire female employees to achieve certain hiring goals. One of the negative outcomes of the increase in female production employees in our plant was the increase in incidents of impropriety between male and female employees.

The whole Harrison Radiator plant fiasco may not have been an error but a calculated plan to thin out the female population in manufacturing. Based on the fact that they did not want to go the thirty miles one way to work and refused the offer, they were dropped from the callback lists. Of the few that did hire in, like my acquaintance, GM simply let them go. By the time spring rolled into Buffalo, there were only a few females remaining in the production area of our plant.

Chapter 7:
UNION JOB ACTIONS—AN ATTEMPT TO SAVE JOBS

It was Saturday, January 7, 1978, and all three shifts of our model shop had a partial crew scheduled for overtime. I was blown away when I arrived to find out that *all* of our skilled trade employees scheduled to work that day had called in sick—my third-shift guys included. All of the supervisors were immediately put on twelve-hour days as if it would even be possible for us to maintain production by ourselves. It was said that the union took this action over layoff notices given to four of our journeymen model makers. I thought the new third-shift work rules also played into the equation.

The union wanted all of their hours cut back to 37.5 a week, thereby saving the four employees from being laid off. Even though our management group would be in favor of eliminating the overlap of shifts, which was unproductive in my mind, something like that would have to be addressed nationally because of the short workweek provisions in the labor agreement between General Motors and the Patternmakers League of North America, who represented them.

On Monday, January 9, at five in the morning, I and the department head were beginning disciplinary interviews with eight third-shift employees. That put the total at forty-three disciplinary actions across the three shifts, but the terms of the discipline were not known as yet. It was rumored that the

GM area manufacturing manager told the casting plant that if another job action took place, all involved would be fired.

On Wednesday, all the employees that were absent the previous Saturday were given the balance of their shift plus three days off with no pay, and two weeks were removed from their length of employment in their personnel records. One of the guys was so upset that the plant nurse sent him to the hospital for blood pressure issues. Some of the younger guys on the second shift were almost in a state of shock upon receiving their time off.

I felt that they had been sold a bill of goods by the union representatives, who likely told them there would be no consequences from the action. Oh well, live and learn, I say! The most important fact was that this was the first time our shop management held their ground and established that the company and not the union ran the operation.

The next day, the twelfth of January, was my birthday which came and went quietly. I can tell you there were no "Happy Birthday" wishes for me that day. It also was obvious that the guys on the second shift were in slowdown mode, still obstinate, and not rationally thinking about where their paychecks came from. Then, on the following Friday, as the day shift began to arrive for work, our supervisory group was alerted that the union had placed an article in the Buffalo newspaper, the *Courier-Express*, titled "Overtime Sick Call Repeat Threatened." The date was, of all days, Friday the thirteenth, January 1978.

Near the end of my shift, I had only three employees committed to the Saturday overtime schedule, so our department head came in at around 5:30 a.m. to address the matter, and he wasn't very happy about it. He immediately asked those three employees about their desire to be scheduled for the Saturday overtime and obtained their verbal commitment. The next four candidates were brought in one at a time, according to seniority and accrued overtime hours, and were told they were required to work Saturday overtime.

It was said that the main reason for the action was that the union members did not think it was right to work overtime while union brothers were laid off. Little did they know that those who were laid off were not going to be called back, and it was a good bet that many more would be laid off in the months to come.

Below are four articles from the *Buffalo Courier-Express* daily newspaper, dated January 13–16, 1978, regarding the actions of the Patternmakers League of North America.

To the best of my recollection, this was the only time this small union ever conducted a job action like that one. It was not only pure desperation but also a case of not fully understanding the gravity of the situation they found themselves in. However, once the union body understood that the company was committed to what it had to do, their attitude began to settle into a realization that their futures may be in jeopardy and there was nothing they could do about it.

Overtime 'Sick Call' 1/13/78
Repeat Is Threatened

By JOE WILHELM
Courier-Express Staff Reporter

A sick call last Saturday by Chevrolet Tonawanda patternmakers has resulted in suspensions for 43 men who refused to work overtime after four other workers were laid off Friday. Another sick call may come this Saturday.

The wildcat action was taken by all but three of the patternmakers scheduled to work overtime last Saturday.

The Patternmakers League of North America, Buffalo Vicinity, which represents 107 patternmakers at the River Road metal casting plant, disclaims any sanction for the action.

Review Due Today

Chevrolet management and the patternmakers shop chairmen were scheduled to meet today to review the situation.

Workers took the action, sources said, because they felt Chevy should use a contract clause to work a shortened work week and avoid layoffs.

Dennis Maria, business agent for the union, said the company stand was that a shortened week was the company's option.

Paul Banyi, league president, said his men "cannot understand why we need overtime after laying off four people. The men were willing to work 7½ hours instead of 8 so the others would not be laid off and then they would be willing to work Saturday."

Not Sanctioned By Union

A four-hour meeting Thursday of patternmakers at Manley's Restaurant on Tonawanda St. reaffirmed the men's intentions to stage another call-in this Saturday unless the situation changes, The Courier-Express learned.

Banyi and Maria reiterated that the league has not sanctioned any actions and declined to comment on a possible repeat. Union officials did report last Saturday.

Three-day suspensions are scheduled to start Monday for the 43 who failed to report last Saturday and will be staggered, about seven at a time, Maria said.

Jerome P. Bishop, regional public relations manager for General Motors Corp., confirmed "a discipline problem" and added "it is still being discussed by management and union."

Saturday is not a normal workday for the patternmakers but the company's position is that employees are supposed to work reasonable overtime, one league spokesman said. He added that the suspensions were issued because the men did "not having a good excuse for not reporting."

Patternmakers make, repair and alter patterns for metal castings for engines.

January 13, 1978 newspaper article about union job action.

Union Urges 34 Men Go Back to Work

1/14/78

Patternmakers at Chevrolet's town of Tonawanda metalcasting plant are expected to take the advice of their international union and report to work this morning, a union official said Friday.

Last Saturday, 43 men called in sick because, sources said, the men were asked to work overtime after four other workers were laid off on the previous Friday.

As a result of the wildcat action, the men received three-day suspensions.

Denis Maria, business agent for The Patternmakers League of North America, Buffalo vicinity, which represents 107 patternmakers at the River Road plant said Friday:

''The international representative of the Patternmakers of North America called and directed me to advise the men that they must work overtime in this instance because the company stated on the reprimand that any further action would result in the immediate discharge of the men involved.''

He added that Wilfred McMarland, the international representative in Pittsburgh, told the area union to grieve the three day layoff under normal grievance procedures.

The union will put in another formal grievance because they believe the company should have allowed the other workers to work 7½ hours instead of 8 so the four men would have not been laid off, Maria said.

Although the men will probably show up for work today, Maria said they "still feel it is morally wrong to work overtime while other employees are being laid off."

Patternmakers make, repair and alter patterns for metal castings for engines.

January 14, 1978 newspaper article urging union members back to work.

Patternmakers Heed Leaders, Work Overtime

1/15/78

BUFFALO

Patternmakers scheduled for overtime work Saturday in the Chevrolet metal-casting plant in the Town of Tonawanda heeded the advice of their union leaders and reported to their jobs.

A group of them on Jan. 7 called in "sick" when they were put on overtime after four other patternmakers had been laid off. There was threat of another "sick" call-in Saturday, but heads of the Patternmakers League of North America advised the craftsmen to go to work.

As a result of the Jan. 7 episode, the company invoked disciplinary procedures against the absentees. The work-schedule dispute is being discussed by the union and employer.

January 15, 1978 newspaper article – Patternmakers Heed Leaders, Work Overtime.

Men Avoid New Fine; Back on Job

1/16/78

Patternmakers at Chevrolet's town of Tonawanda metal casting plant reported to work Saturday on the advice of their international union.

Dennis Maria, business agent for the Pattern Makers of North America, said the men reported rather than be fined with another three day suspension.

Last Saturday, 43 men from the Tonawanda plant called in sick because they were asked to work overtime following the layoff of four of their fellow workers. They were given a three day suspension which begins today as a result of their action.

"We hope to have another meeting with the corporation sometime this week." Maria said. "We are looking for reduced work time and the restoration of four men's jobs.

January 16, 1978 newspaper article – Men Avoid New Fine; Back on the job.

59

Chapter 8:
HEAVY MANUFACTURING—A DANGEROUS ENVIRONMENT

To this day, people believe that employees working in an automobile plant have cushy jobs and that they are overpaid for what they do. When these same folks enter their vehicles and turn the key in the ignition switch—or in more advanced vehicles, push a button—the engine starts and off they go with no earthly idea of the complexity of the design and engineering and all the difficult, dangerous, and tedious work that takes place within the manufacturing and assembly plants and those of suppliers.

It appears to me that consumers never give employees credit for their labor, but they fully trust the vehicle when making an extremely sharp turn on a winding road, making an emergency stop to avoid a life-threatening situation, or simply cruising down the interstate going eighty miles an hour and feeling oh so confident and safe. Some of this may be linked to how the public views unions and how they have evolved into a political machine. But that is not what this book is about.

Since all my work history in General Motors was accrued at the Tonawanda Metal Casting Plant, the following accounts are from my notes and recollections from that facility exclusively.

As described earlier in the book, the plant where I worked was a metal casting plant whose cast-iron products included engine blocks, cylinder heads, exhaust manifolds, intake manifolds, brake drums, and fly wheels. At the back end of the plant was the melting department, where two cupolas were used to melt the materials to approximately 2,500 degrees Fahrenheit. From the cupolas, the molten iron was released into large holding ladles for distribution to the molding lines.

Now, to get the molten iron from there to the pouring stations at the end of each of the molding lines, of which our plant had eight, we had an overhead monorail system. On it rode "iron cars" toting a bucket holding up to two tons of molten cast iron and its human operator. The operators of the transfer cars would position the bucket under the spout of one of the holding ladles, which tilted and poured molten iron into the bucket of the transfer car. At that time, the operators always stayed in their compartments and at the controls while this was going on. Once the bucket was filled, they went on their way to deliver to a line.

With this brief background, just imagine what happened one weekday in the late afternoon: One of our operators positioned his overhead transfer car to allow the molten iron to fill it. Another unit came up behind the one being filled, and when that operator attempted to stop his unit, the brakes failed, and it bumped the car in front of him. This bump pushed the unit being filled directly under the flow of molten iron and was dropping on top of the roof of the operator's compartment and flowing over it to the floor below.

Those at the scene of this horrific accident believed that if the operator would have stayed put in his compartment (easier said than done), it might not have been too bad. However, he panicked and jumped several feet to the concrete floor beneath him. The problem was that the iron had coated the floor around the area, and it was as slippery as grease. The guy slipped a few times before losing his balance and fell face down in the stuff. He was heroically rescued from that awful position and placed up against a wall to wait for medical assistance and transfer to the hospital.

I did not see this as it happened but was told he was burnt to a crisp. He had to be a very tough individual, because he survived for two days. I can't even begin to imagine how painful and shocking this was for this employee and his family.

Another incident took place in the core room, where the process involved a sand mixture being blown into the two-part tooling under very high air pressure. This particular day, an operator made an unsafe reach across the open halves of tooling while it was in automatic mode. His arm got caught in the tooling as it slammed shut, and the sand was then blown into the tooling and his arm. His arm was unmercifully flattened, and when the tooling opened up, he took off running down an aisle, screaming in pain. A friend of mine, a general supervisor of inspection, ran him down, tackled him, and called for first aide, the plant nurse, and the ambulance. The man was never seen in the plant again.

This next story comes from the finishing department, which was one of the roughest areas of the plant, not only in the type of work that was performed but also the type of personality that filled those positions. As it was told, on the second shift, a newly hired supervisor got into a dispute with his crew about him administrating break times "according to the book." It was eerily similar to the situation in my department regarding the length of lunch and break times.

The bottom line was that both the medical and the plant security people were called. Though it was said that the supervisor sustained a brutal cut to his face from a fall, it appeared that his face had been cut by a sharp item. Things were quiet for a while until rumors circulated that he had been assaulted and cut by one of his subordinates.

About a week or so after the incident, a nurse who was working in the emergency room at the local hospital that evening told me that when the supervisor was brought in, it appeared that the wound had been made by an extremely sharp instrument that had cut him from the corner of his mouth through his entire cheek. She told us it was the worst cut she'd ever seen, period. This supervisor's career at GM ended, and I imagine he was never the same after the attack.

Once each year the plant went on shutdown to get ready for the new model year. Equipment repairs were undertaken, and tooling was changed or upgraded. Often outside contractors were brought in to do major facility revisions. During one of these shutdowns, a situation ended in a fatality for one of the hired contractors. He was an iron worker revising some of the steel structure high above the production floor in the molding area. I did not hear of the particulars, but I do know that as he fell, he bounced off beams on the way down and died on the plant floor. It was gruesome and sad, and though he was not an employee of GM, it was a very sad day for our facility.

The last incident I will describe did not take place in the plant but at the United Auto Workers' business office, which was just a block away from the property in a single-family home the union was renting. In the middle of the day, while the treasurer was at his desk performing his duties, an armed man came in and robbed and shot him. He died from his wounds. I don't know if the case was ever solved.

I should mention that these five incidents were but a few of the many incidents and accidents that took place during my eighteen years at GM, which included many employees being run into by fork trucks, receiving bad cuts, and sustaining broken bones.

I hope that the accounts of these incidents give you, the consumer, a better understanding and appreciation for those working at General Motors and other automobile manufacturers, as well as the entire US manufacturing workforce.

MADE IN THE USA!

Chapter 9:

QUALITY OF WORK LIFE—A GREAT EXPERIENCE WHILE IT LASTED

It was early 1978. For some time, Japanese auto companies had been gaining momentum in America. Because of this, General Motors had managers from all of their many casting plants and other areas take a trip to visit Japanese production facilities to "find out how they were doing it."

When they came back from this educational visit, our representative presented a grim picture of our competitors and what we were up against. In meetings with salaried employees he explained Japanese work conditions in regard to wages, safety, the environment, and employee commitment. You could tell by his words and tone that he was concerned that it would be a difficult road ahead for us, because General Motors Corporation and other US manufacturers were spending a lot of money cleaning up their plants on the inside and the outside to be responsible to their workers and to the environment. But Japanese manufacturers, like Chinese manufacturers today, didn't have to comply with government regulations like US industry did. Also, their employees' wages were very low, and they had to work in unsafe conditions.

General Motors Corporation had also been hearing for some time about the Quality Circles that Japanese automakers were using in their plants as a way to involve their workers in the process. The direct result of that was the formation of the GM Quality of Work Life (QWL) process. It was a big deal. Each plant appointed a QWL coordinator, who would be trained by corporate personnel staff to bring the process to the individual plants. Our plant wasn't in the first wave of facilities to implement it, but upper management developed a plant outline, and a steering committee made up of plant staff began the process.

On October 2, 1978, while working on the first shift, I was called into our department head's office, where he informed me that I had been chosen to be the plant's QWL coordinator for our 2,500-employee facility. This was a complete shock to me, as I had not asked for it; I didn't even know they were looking for someone to fill this important position. He said that he felt it was "a very good opportunity for my career." From there we walked downstairs to talk to the second-shift general production superintendent, who was to be the chairman of the program. From that first meeting, I could tell he was a super guy. He also told me that this was an opportunity, but that there were "no promises" and that I would begin the position on October 15, 1978.

This was a big deal for me, as it was the first time I'd had such a huge responsibility thrown at me. It meant training the entire management group once I had learned what the QWL process was all about. Even though I was ready to take on the responsibility, I did have some anxiety. No one, including me, knew much about this new GM program or what would be involved.

Once the dust settled over the announcement, it was concluded that I would be working out of the personnel department on "special assignment" during the week and in the shop over the weekends "as needed." All kinds of thoughts ran through my mind about how my boss in the shop and the supervisors I worked with were going to take this news. Because of how they'd handled my school situation in the past, I thought their reactions might be a little negative. It would not be long before I found out.

A week later I was to be in Ann Arbor, Michigan with a member of the plant staff, attending a Quality of Work Life Familiarization Session. I could just imagine how Mac was carrying on about how he could not run the shop with one less supervisor.

October 15 was an overtime Saturday that happened to be thirteen days since the announcement that I would be the QWL coordinator. Just prior to our lunch period, Mac told me that the shop couldn't afford to let me go as planned. I responded to his comment by saying, "I am not in a position to reverse what has already been directed by my new boss," which was the plant manager. I also told him, "If that is what you want, you had better discuss it with the general production superintendent." Later in the shift, Mac told me that on Monday I would have a meeting with my department head and the two general production superintendents.

This incident only proved my suspicions that a few of my management team were quite uncomfortable with my recent assignment and possible good fortune. I thought that this was not the path a successful business should be on to be competitive in the world market.

At 2:30 p.m. on Monday, October 17, the day of the meeting between me and the brass, I had not heard anything except what Mac had told me earlier in the day: that our department head had stated he would not let me go until the current temporary supervisor was promoted to permanent. Here we had the department head, two steps above my general supervisor, who had somehow been dragged into this stall tactic to get another supervisor on permanent status.

Since there was no indication of a meeting taking place, I went downstairs and asked the second-shift production superintendent, also the QWL chairman, when the meeting was. He had not heard of any such meeting, which meant an out-and-out lie had been put out there to delay the inevitable. He told me he would find out what was going on.

Three days later, on October 20th, the first-shift production superintendent came up to our department to talk to my department head, for reasons unknown to me. As he was leaving, I said, "Good morning," and he replied with the same. He was out the door when he suddenly turned around and walked back into the office, where I was reviewing the shop log. He sat down in a chair off to the side of the desk and asked, "If you were to start right away on the QWL assignment, what would I be doing?" Because I had been preparing for the position on my own time, I immediately ran off a half-dozen items, and he nodded. Then he left. Only a short time later, the phone rang and I was summoned to his production office.

When I arrived, he cut to the chase, saying, "The plant manager wanted me to begin immediately, and that means now." I said that I would not get much done in the last two hours, but if that was what he wanted, that was what I would do. I believe what happened was that the plant manager, a former US Marine, was thinking I was already set up in the personnel department, and he was upset with the delay.

I went back to the shop and told my general supervisor what had just gone down, and the blood drained from his face. It was finally evident to him that the delaying tactics were no longer going to be in play, and they would have to move ahead without me. Like the place would shut down without me? Right! So it was looking like I'd have at least one year as QWL coordinator in the personnel department on weekdays and as supervisor in the shop on weekends "as needed."

A week later I was in Ann Arbor for two days devoted to learning the entire scope and goals of the corporate QWL process and how the corporation expected the coordinators to proceed in their respective units. This would involve using corporate guidelines of the process and tweaking them to be in tune with the needs of our plant and employees. It would also require personally training the entire management team with a one-week, off-site class as well as organizing Quality Circles for the hourly workforce to get involved in a direct way. That would be followed up with moving the process into the plant for the hourly workforce. It was scary to think of being the one who would be responsible for this endeavor in a 2,500-person plant. I would be answering to the second-shift production manager and the plant manager. Was I in for a surprise?

One morning during the following week, the plant manager stopped into my office (actually it was the second-shift production manager's, who had allowed me to use it). He began a conversation aimed at making me feel comfortable and getting a feel for me and my plans for the program. Toward the end of the ten-minute exchange, he said, "I really don't know how to put this, but it looks as though you may have been held back in the model shop." Then he went on to say, "Do a good job with this QWL program, and maybe there will be something for you in the future with the corporation." I told him thanks, and he left the room.

The plant manager was the third and most influential person who had told me substantially the same thing, and I knew that the person who held the QWL position at the forge plant in our complex was now a superintendent and later, after I was "separated" by GM in 1981 ("given my marching papers," "pink slipped," call it what you want), the plant manager at the River Road Motor Plant.

This is a very good time to quickly explain that I was selected for this position out of all salaried employees in the plant. The selection process was done by a committee including the plant manager and the entire staff. I often asked myself how I was chosen. I rationalized that it was because I had seventeen years of service, went back to school for my bachelor's degree, and stood tall during the difficult times with my department's work rules. Still, someone in this staff management group would have had to bring up my name as a potential candidate.

Early in January of 1979, while attending my next-door neighbor's house party, I discovered what I thought could be the elusive answer to my being thrown into the mix. The plant manager used to live on my street, his sister still lived on that street, and he had his vehicles taken care of at a shop owned by one of the party attendees. Could that have put my name on the radar screen? All of these things were coincidences, and maybe there wasn't any connection. But the last item that came out in the discussion at the party was that the plant manager was an alumnus of Buffalo State, where I had earned my degree. Although this could have been the clue I was looking for, I never found out the real reason.

Things seemed to smooth out for the next month or so, with me developing an official outline for the plant as a guide to implement the QWL process, attending all staff meetings, and building a rapport with managers, supervisors, and hourly production workers, as well as working some Saturdays in the shop.

The next month and a half flew by, and before I knew it, the holiday shutdown (Christmas 1978 and New Year 1979) began. In the blink of an eye, a new year was upon us, along with the expectation of how successful I would be when this process moved forward and how it might impact the casting plant and my career in the years to come.

1979—QUALITY OF WORK LIFE, TWENTY-FIVE YEAR PLANT ANNIVERSARY, AND TROUBLE IS LURKING

The plant was in its first days of being back to work after the long (almost two weeks), paid Christmas break. I happened to stop by the shop, looking to say hello to the management team, and almost immediately ran into my general supervisor. There was no "how was your holiday," but he did tell me how swamped he was and how he may need to "borrow me" for about three weeks. He had to know that would not be possible, so why even utter such nonsense, especially when he was the third person in charge in the department and earning approximately 45,000 a year at the time.

Since my position as Quality of Work Life coordinator was considered a staff position, I would be present at all plant staff meetings, where I would give a brief progress report on the program. However, what I had been witnessing was the inability of the staff to get things resolved. It reminded me of a soap opera. You could miss a couple of meetings, and when you returned the same production-killing items were being mulled over and over.

I do not know what the others, including the plant manager, were thinking, but I was worried about how this lack of management action was going to bite us all in the near future. It was also worrisome that even though we were getting information on casting orders coming in, management was acting all excited about orders for brake drums, which simply could not support our plant. For our plant to stay in business, we needed to be casting cylinder blocks, cylinder heads, and intake and exhaust manifolds. I believe the staff was fully aware of this, even though the shop superintendent was attempting to paint a bright picture for the attendees. It was a trifle embarrassing.

A few days later, on January 11, 1979, at a morning staff meeting, the salaried personnel director read a letter announcing that eighty-six salaried employees were being laid off, effective at the end of the month. Of course, this wasn't what anyone wanted to hear to begin a new year, and it would certainly place more responsibility and strain on the fortunate employees who avoided the cut.

Later that day I was clearing the desk of the second-shift

superintendent, which I had been using. When he came in we discussed how terribly the plant had been running. He was noticeably concerned about what it would take to remedy all the issues in order to turn the plant around.

The following day, January 12, 1979, was my thirty-sixth birthday, and it turned out to be just another trying day for me at the plant. The QWL steering committee had a scheduled meeting today, and I had put in a big effort in producing a handout for the attendees, including staff members, to show them how the program was progressing. When the meeting was over, I sat in the room by myself, totally discouraged by what had taken place.

First, the plant manager could not attend—no reason given, of course. Second, there were no comments of any substance from any of the attendees to indicate any interest or excitement regarding this important corporate mission. Third, in the middle of the meeting, two people were called out because of production issues. Finally, and most disturbing of all, when the meeting was adjourned and all the managers had left, I found several of my handouts on the chairs. It showed me right then and there that I and the corporation would have a difficult road ahead in implementing this new way of doing business, especially at the Tonawanda Metal Casting Plant.

MY APPRAISAL, OH MY!

Because I had been patiently waiting for over a month for my appraisal to be prepared, reviewed, signed, and turned in, I went to the appropriate person in the personnel department to express my frustration with the situation. After all, it was already the sixteenth of January of 1978, and it should have been completed by the first of December. However, not one of my bosses in the shop had mentioned anything to indicate that they knew it still needed to be done.

Even though I was on special assignment status in the personnel department, only working weekends in the model shop as required, the powers that be had decided that my model shop supervisor would handle my appraisal. Now, how in the heck could that be? It would be like me doing an employee review for a production worker on a molding line. Ridiculous, yes, but that was the GM way.

The person in personnel asked me who was to handle my appraisal. As soon as I told him, and with me standing there, he called the shop and told Mac to "hurry up on this one." He hung up the phone and told me to let him know if it didn't happen. I thanked him for his effort and thought how pissed Mac would be because of my action.

Four days had passed since the phone call to Mac, and I was working an overtime Saturday in the shop with him. Remarkably, he did not mention anything to me about my appraisal, and without having it completed would have a direct influence on the Merit Increase System and therefore would have a marked effect on my salary. This would affect not only me but also my family. In retrospect, I believe that this was why I was so upset with Mac, who basically did not give a damn about it, even though it was his responsibility. I felt like he wanted me to beg him for it, but I just kept my cool and did the best job I could for the department.

The following Monday, January 22, 1979, I ran into him in the production area and casually asked if he had my appraisal ready. To my surprise and amazement, he said that he had not worked on it yet. I told him in a nice way that it was important to me to get it done, and that was the end of the exchange. I was thinking of taking the situation to the department head but decided to take a wait-and-see stance a while longer. I would bet that I was not the only person in the plant experiencing the irresponsibility of supervisors.

On January 26, there was still no indication that my appraisal was any closer to being ready. I decided to discuss it once again with the salaried personnel department. I told my contact that I would be out of the plant for a one-week training class in Ann Arbor for the QWL program, and I made it clear that when I returned on February 5, I expected my appraisal to be ready to go. If it would be done then, it would be sixty days past my appraisal due date.

My panic and disgust related back to the first supervisor review/appraisal Bill gave me. At that time, even though I was doing all that was asked of me, including running the shop alone at times with zero indications of incompetence, my review was crappy. That's being nice about it. He didn't even fill out half of the cover sheet, and how he got away with turning in such a deplorable document I don't know. This is one of the many reasons for me writing this book. I still can't believe I signed that damned thing. I knew that if my next merit increase was influenced at all by it, I would take a hit in the pocketbook, which would have an impact on my family. That's what upset me the most.

Fast-forward a week. I returned to the plant after the weeklong training in Ann Arbor. I knew I was back in the real world of GM when I was told that Mac had been forced to give personnel my appraisal over the phone with the written document to follow. Remember that this was to be done by my anniversary date of December 1, 1978, and on February 6, 1979, he had given only a verbal review to personnel.

The bottom line is that I eventually had my review, even though it was not what I had hoped for. Think about it. I was chosen for the QWL position special assignment over the entire salaried workforce at our location, and while working on that huge project I kept myself up to speed in the shop by working weekends as needed (almost all of them). Unbelievably, my supervisor used this as an excuse not to rate me higher than he did, saying that because I was on this special assignment, I had not been able to keep up with all that was going on.

That was a total lie, and I should have challenged the appraisal and taken it higher up. However, because I was so tired of the whole fiasco, I signed it. And the rest is history. Also, and no surprise to me, there were others in the department with very late appraisals. It was very difficult to have a supervisor who was so negligent and incompetent rating my performance and then having to go out into the plant to try to improve the quality of work life for the entire plant. Oh my!

BACK TO QUALITY OF WORK LIFE

Back in late January of 1979, a staff member of our plant and I, along with two representatives of the motor plant, met on a Sunday and drove to Ann Arbor for the weeklong Quality of Work Life Facilitators Workshop. (There were five plants in the complex: a motor machining and assembly plant, a casting plant, a forge plant, and a plant that machined and assembled cylinder heads. They had a total of about ten thousand employees.) Even though this was the best work experience I ever encountered, including meeting and interacting with high-quality and well-intentioned people, it was nevertheless an eye opener to me to see the disconnect between the corporate personnel folks and the real world as I and those at the Tonawanda Metal Casting Plant lived it.

During the week we found out about the core of the program and did many group exercises to get us used to the program we were expected to implement back at our plants. This event was well executed and answered all my questions pertaining to the program's depth and seriousness as well as what my responsibility would be in establishing and moving it through our 2,500-person facility.

Upon returning to the real world, I began working hard on

developing a strategy that included Quality Circles in which hourly production and skilled trades folks were invited to sit down to discuss better ways to get the job done. Also going into high gear was planning and rehearsing for the eight-hour, off-site workshop geared to introduce the QWL program to *all* salaried personnel.

Then, toward the end of February, I noticed that I was being asked by more than one staff person to do this or to do that for them. It wasn't like my job as QWL coordinator didn't keep me busy, as I did have a mandated timing for implementing the program. So how was I to fulfill all of those extra requests?

As an example, since I was to be involved in our plant's twenty-fifth anniversary open house, the staff member who was overseeing the event asked me to write a letter scheduling the planning meeting. That was pure buck passing. Then a month later I was assigned to coordinate the Savings Plan Campaign (US bonds) for the hourly workforce. On the surface, it did not look difficult, but when I opened the packet prepared by the Central Office staff in Saginaw, I discovered that everything was to be in motion by March 19.

It was already April 9, and as usual they were kicking the can down the road until something had to be done, and I was the lucky one to get stuck with it. Two days later I received a note from this guy in personnel that since he would be going on vacation the following week, I would be handling the Salaried Payroll Savings Plan alone. I was really ticked off and thought that he did this very underhandedly, as we had talked the day before and he had not said a word about his vacation.

If this was not bad enough, I was asked to work in the shop Thursday, Friday, and Saturday, which just happened to be Easter weekend. It was obvious that when the clique in my department found an opportunity to benefit themselves, I was deemed prepared enough to run the shop alone. This really sucked, because it did not have to be this way. My family and I survived, and all I could do was move on.

Then on April 10, 1979, because the plant had been running so poorly for a month and a half, I was informed that the QWL budget, which began at 40,000 dollars for the year, was being cut to 25,000, even though it had always been the corporate stance that the program would go on regardless of any business unit's challenges.

I was shaken to the core to hear, at the end of the day, that the budget was officially cut to *zero*. So much for the commitment. And I wondered how this would be viewed by Central Office. I also wondered how it was going to affect me. Was my position going to be terminated, or would I continue to have the opportunity to make a difference at our location? Since my salary continued to be drawn from the department from which I was borrowed, I thought I would be allowed to continue. And that's exactly what took place.

The next couple of months went by extremely fast while I developed and had in-plant Quality Circle meetings with production people; worked on the upcoming eight-hour QWL offsite workshop presentation for all salaried employees, including the development of slides and handouts; planned and arranged for the plant's twenty-fifth anniversary open house; coordinated the hourly and salaried employees Payroll Savings Plans; and last but not least, worked in conjunction with the forge plant, which was part of our manufacturing complex, in developing a twenty-five-year employee service memento and program.

In mid-June of 1979, the push to get me out of the plush office I was sharing with the second-shift production superintendent was intensifying. I never did find out where this was coming from, but I was instructed to set up shop in the Suggestion Office, even though there was no desk for me. When a desk was finally delivered, it was so bad that everyone had a good laugh, even though it was a disgrace that an item such as it was not in the trash. Its drawers were not in operating condition, the paint was badly chipped, and it had a leg missing, so they propped it up with a block of wood. I could not make this up. This actually took place in a facility of one of the greatest car companies in the world.

Over the next few days, I was able to locate and procure a desk that was in slightly better condition, but I never did get a phone for the duration of my tenure in the QWL assignment. I was told that this was because all available phone line extensions were taken, and it would be too costly to pull another cable from the motor plant. Consequently I had to use the phone in the office I had been sharing to make calls, and incoming calls for me came through the general office number with no answering machine for messages. Just great!

It was the morning of June 19, 1979, when I was summoned to the plant manager's office. It was always sort of weird to sit down with him, because once you were in, he would close the double doors with a push of a button on his desk. There were charts all over the walls with all sorts of production statistics as well as an electrical display with a schematic of all the molding lines; lights would come on whenever equipment went down during production.

He said he wanted to talk to me about some changes for our twenty-fifth anniversary open house that I had been working on for almost six months. He now wanted a memento for special guests of the open house. I told him that I would look at some options and report back to him. He also dropped this next item in my lap: the forge plant was going to have an open house along with ours, and I would be coordinating it along with the 25 Year Service Awards Recognition Luncheon for approximately one hundred employees from both plants.

I didn't have the nerve to tell him that these additional items would be difficult to accomplish, given the time constraints and also the fact that I did not have a phone at my desk. The big day was at the end of August, but the exact date escapes me. I was excused, the doors began to open, and I left the office.

In the next couple of weeks, for mementos I was able to have the guys in the model shop make wood shields made with a miniature V8 cast-iron engine block and engraved brass. I also had an outside vendor provide us with prototype cocktail glasses with a silver coating and white inscription. Across the top was "Tonawanda Metal Casting" with the "bowtie" at either end. In script at the lower part was "Silver Anniversary," and in the middle "1954–1979." I still have one.

In addition I was having huge banners that would be hung on the side of the building; a magician was lined up; local Chevy dealers were going to bring new vehicles on the grounds for display; and there would be games for the kids and handouts for all. This was not the entire program but the main items. By the end of July, even though I had asked everyone short of the plant manager, I was still managing without a phone on my desk.

A week and a half later, on August 1, 1979, the plant manager called me into his office. Once again I had that weird feeling as the double doors closed behind me. In retrospect, what he was about to tell me was the first definitive sign of big trouble at this plant and for General Motors as a whole.

He told me that, because of declining sales, the corporation had informed all managers to stop all "unnecessary" expenditures. Because of that, he had to put a stop to the open house event, even though it had been worked on for the last six months and was only three and a half weeks away. I was stunned by this order; all the planning, lining up of vendors, and sending out of invitations had all been for naught. I felt, and not just because I had a major role in this project, that this open house was going to put our plant on the map in the community as well as in the corporation. He buzzed the doors open, and I left his office stunned by what had just taken place.

As I sat at my desk, it was difficult for me to see how it was looked at as an unnecessary expenditure. After all, you can have a silver anniversary only once, and there had already been a good sum of money spent up to that point. I immediately began to call all the vendors to advise them to stop where they were and bill us accordingly. Those were the most uncomfortable calls I had ever made. I also had to send out one hundred letters of regret to all of the VIP invitees.

The bottom line was that the plant was stuck with 5,200 dollars' worth of mementos, 2,500 balloons, 8,000 cookies, 2,500 press-on designs for kids' T-shirts, and approximately 2,000 dollars in signs and placards—not to mention the wages paid during the past six months. The second-shift manufacturing manager and I passed all these items out to employees, and that was that. I was then able to focus fully on the QWL program and the upcoming offsite seminars for the salaried employees.

The next day I happened to be talking with our plant safety supervisor, and he told me that when he brought up the subject of the open house cancellation and all the work that went into it, the personnel director had replied that "not much had been done." This was an absurd comment but it did not come as a complete surprise to me. My supervisor in the shop as well as my supervisor in the personnel department felt that they were the only ones who had anything to do in the place.

On August 31, 1979, fourteen salaried employees were released and three in production management were dropped down a level (with a pay cut), while at the same time the General Motors Corporation handed out the largest Cost of Living Allowance (COLA) checks (by UAW contract) in the history of General Motors. However, on that Friday my thoughts were centered on whether I would survive another cut, and if so, whether I would be out the door or sent back to my department.

I had been working on a letter to announce the upcoming QWL offsite workshops, which included the logistics, scheduling procedure, and goals of the program. On September 12, I took it to the plant personnel director for review. I wrote this letter after having an opportunity to read a similar letter penned by the plant manager of the motor plant, which I improved on. It was interesting that in the motor plant the manager wrote this announcement letter, but my plant had me, the QWL coordinator, produce it.

My boss, the personnel director, read it out loud while I stood in his office, and then he said, "This is okay. This is good. But I would like you to put in a little more information about the program. You know what I mean." So even though I had improved on the motor plant manager's letter and even though he did not have anything specific to contribute, he had to pull rank and have me go back and revise it. But how, and with what? I had never taken anything to this guy without him giving me an initial okay. I always had to revise and go back for his approval, even if only for some inconsequential reason. I made a revision, and the letter was approved and finally distributed.

About a week later, the plant grapevine had it that there was to be another cut of salaried employees to take place on October 1. The plant continued cutting employees, even though we were short-staffed to begin with. We had to wonder what the grand scheme was for this plant and our future.

The morning of October 12, 1979, had me at the General Motors Training Center in Clarence, a suburb of Buffalo, where I was going through a dry run of the eight-hour program I would be presenting to the entire salaried workforce for the next three weeks. A coworker from personnel was to join me to help in this process. Not only did the original person not show up, but his backup didn't show either.

I went through all of the material and all of the slides without my co-workers present. Incredibly, as I was wrapping things up around the noon hour, one of the no-shows called me from the plant and said he was assigned to assist me with the first week of sessions and wanted to review the program I had set up. After waiting almost an hour for him to arrive, we reviewed for the remainder of the day.

Late in the afternoon, the salaried personnel supervisor called and began screaming about the interim United Way campaign report. I assumed that he had been asked by his boss, the personnel director, or the plant manager about it. Here was the co-chairman of the drive with me, who knew full well what would be taking up my time for the next three weeks, having the gall to ask me where the report was.

He was not my supervisor. However, in my position as QWL coordinator, any time a manager needed something and did not have the resources to accomplish it, he would simply call me and have me do it. I once counted twelve people, from the plant manager to my supervisor, in the shop on weekends who could technically be called my boss, because I had to answer to most of their whims. That was not what this position was meant to be. My job was to get the plant working as a team and developing an environment in which the employees would have some ownership through their own ideas and suggestions for process improvements or safety. It was not going as envisioned.

We finally wrapped up the review process and made our way back to the plant. Rather than going home for the day, I stayed over until 6:30 p.m. and completed the report that the co-chairman could not fit into his busy day. From what I could see from the signup sheets, it looked like there would be only ten salaried employees for the first day of classes; at least that many had to cancel because of a variety of plant and personal issues. My thought was that it would be nice to see a show of commitment by management, or anyone else for that matter, regarding the QWL process. Dreamin'.

Monday, October 15, 1979, marked the beginning of the QWL offsite seminars, and I have to say that the days leading up to the opening day and the morning introduction were very nerve-wracking times for me. However, because of all the training provided by the corporation and all the prep work I had put into the program, I did just fine, even with a simple outline at hand.

When Murphy's Law sprang up early in the day and the tape machine decided it did not want to cooperate, I knew the class would not hear the "Massey Tapes," which were the corporation's way of kicking off the program. But I didn't have a meltdown. With my notes I was able to complete that part of the introduction well. The day went great, and the attendees received the QWL message positively. Anything positive at that point in the plant's history was quite welcome. The negative of the day was the fact that we had ten no-shows.

By the completion of the first week, the attendance had improved dramatically, although I'm not sure why. I shuddered to think that if I had twelve each week miss the class, we'd have over thirty salaried employees missing this very important step in the process. That would be a difficult scenario when we attempted to move forward on the plant floor.

As the days went by, I improved my delivery to the point that the attendees gave me a round of applause at the conclusion of most of the classes. This totally blew me away, especially when you consider that all they were experiencing in the plant was grief. I believe the positive message was what they were looking for, and they got it. On Thursday, October 25th, and with only one week of classes remaining, I had Mac, my supervisor in the Master Mechanic Department, in attendance. And an incident took place that made my skin crawl.

I had known for some time that, because of the budget issues confronting our plant, once the QWL orientation classes were completed, I would be reporting back to the Master Mechanic Department from which I was borrowed. In my absence, the name of our shop—or department, if you will—was changed from Pattern Shop to the Master Mechanics Department. No clue on how that one came about. The reason such an effort was made to change the name at a time when there were much larger fish to fry still eludes me, but that was GM.

On the morning of October 25, 1979, while class attendees were arriving and getting coffee and a doughnut, I was greeting them and welcoming them to the class. When Mac arrived, I approached and greeted him as I had been doing with all the attendees. To my amazement, these were the first words he uttered: "They [all the shop supervision] told upper management that they did not want me back as supervisor if the newest supervisor has to be laid off." I thought, *How is that for a Quality of Work Life good morning, especially from a guy who has been in the same department as me and whom I have worked with for seventeen years.*

Here's what was really going on: During the entire time I had been on this "special assignment opportunity" and even though they had been taking advantage of me by having me cover the shop on most weekends and holidays, this general supervisor had been complaining that he was shorthanded in supervision. He used that to fast-track the temp supervisor in question to a permanent position so that I would be forced out of the shop to another area—or even worse, out the door. This was as ugly as it gets, and it took place while the corporation and the plant were taking great steps to correct actions like it.

I proceeded to deliver another very good presentation, and when the class ended, most of the attendees approached me and complimented me on the class. Mac, not surprisingly, did not.

I spent part of the following day at the training center, gathering some excess items to take back to the plant to begin the process of wrapping up the QWL seminars. I had one week of seminars remaining, and that would be it.

When I arrived at the plant, the two department heads I needed to see were not there, and when I finally ran down our new department head, he immediately expressed resentment regarding my arrival date being Monday, November 5, rather than Thursday, November 1. For God's sake, I wasn't through with the assignment until Friday, November 2, and not two days before that I was being told that "they" did not want me back, and he was upset that I would not be in on the earlier date. I'm absolutely positive that if I started on a Thursday, I would not only be working the weekend but also would be alone most of the evening.

Also, while in his office, and because no one thought it important to tell me, I had to ask the department head what shift I would be working. Not a small point. I guess they assumed I could read their minds. His answer that I would be assigned to the second shift did not surprise me—except for the fact that I was enrolled in night-school at Erie Community College for a metal-casting practices course. I had enrolled in the class at the request of plant management and which they would pay for. So for them to be inconsiderate of our senior plant management was astonishing. When I brought this to his attention, even though his reputation in the plant was that of a fair manager, he suggested I pick up the second semester during the following school year. He knew that I would still be on the evening shift then, so he was basically saying that that particular class was history.

I thought if this was what management's idea of Quality of Work Life was going to be, it would result in plenty of money and effort going down the drain as well as disappointment for the employees as well as the corporate folks. Their treatment of me while I was still the plant Quality of Work Life coordinator told me that the future plans I had in the works, such as QWL Quality Circles, would not see the light of day. And they did not.

I soon heard who would be the "lucky" guy to be the next QWL coordinator. This man already had plenty on his plate. He was a labor representative, he supervised three people covering three phases of the Company Car Program, he was involved in human relations management, and now he was being told, not asked, to take over the QWL coordinator position. There would not be enough time in the day for him to accomplish what needed to be done, which indicated to me that our plant manager had made a conscious decision to slow down the Quality of Work Life process. When I was told that he also demanded from this man a daily written report detailing all his activities, I felt sorry for the poor guy. After all, he already had an overflowing plate; for this plant manager to nitpick this employee was inexcusable.

The plant manager also furloughed three more production clerks, which left our manufacturing group with only one clerk to handle two very large production departments. Keep in mind that there was not a computer at every desk to assist in productivity; typewriters and copiers were all she wrote. All of this was beginning to reveal that serious problems in the economy—along with GM losing market share—had the corporation, and the casting plant in particular, in a lot of trouble. The implications of the manager's actions were serious and scary, and I tried not to dwell on them, because individuals can only do the best they can; the rest would be out of their hands.

The following Monday, October 29, 1979, I began the final week of the Quality of Work Life seminars. It was to be a great week, not only because I had the material down and perfected but also because the attendees had some advance information about the seminar from those who had already attended. I got the feeling that they were ready for changes and that they were willing to give this QWL process a chance. I felt they were ready for improved personal relations in the plant and improved plant performance.

The Monday class was going great until I received a phone call just prior to our lunch break while the attendees were completing an exercise. I thought everyone knew where I was and what I was doing, so I wondered if there was some kind of emergency. I answered the phone. It was my co-chairman for our United Way campaign, who went into his song and dance and whining about the campaign not progressing very well. This was a guy I'd recently had words with about how it was impossible for me to be in two places at one time. He knew that as well as everyone in the plant. The class was waiting for me to wrap up their exercise and break for lunch, so I told him I would talk about it when I returned to the plant.

The class went great, and when I arrived back at the plant, I marched right over to his desk with my coat still on and flat-out told him that it was not professional of him to call me and bitch about the United Way campaign when he knew full well I was in the middle of presenting a QWL seminar. I repeated what I'd told him before: he was co-chairman of the campaign, so he needed to do some of the work while I was out of the plant, period. He was beside himself because he knew full well that I would be returning to my department as a supervisor, and he and my successor would be charged with that rather large undertaking.

Friday, November 2, 1979, was the final day of the Quality of Work Life seminars. In a way, I was not only glad it was over but also very satisfied that I had done an excellent job with the assignment. After each class day, the comments from the attendees had been very uplifting and encouraging. I had the feeling that the experience might open a door for me in General Motors, but more importantly there was a glimmer of hope that this program might change how we did things in our plant.

On this day, class went very well again, and when participants were leaving, I received many handshakes, pats on the shoulder, and comments like "Nice job." When everyone was gone, I collected all the materials and equipment and loaded up the company vehicle.

Rather than going back to our plant, I had to take some borrowed videotapes back to the personnel department of the

Harrison Radiator plant in Lockport. After introductions, I was given a tour of their personnel department. It was a real eye opener to observe the huge difference between their facility and ours. Work areas were clean; there was plenty of room to get jobs done; the conference rooms were out of this world. And they actually had phones at each desk.

While I was driving back to the plant, my thoughts were on how the corporation could expect the same level of employee attitude and pride, and the resulting productivity, in such differing work environments and whether the QWL process would be able to overcome these kinds of hurdles. As I got closer to our plant, I began to feel a little sad that our plant's management had reneged on their commitment by having me go back to the shop and passing the buck to someone who was already swamped. I felt like this cheapened what I had gone through and accomplished.

I had no idea how significant and shocking the following year's experiences would be, not only for me but also for the plant as a whole.

Chapter 10:
BACK TO THE REAL WORLD—GM AFTER QWL

My entire morning and early afternoon while at home on Monday, November 5, 1979, was spent nervously thinking about my return to the second shift in the shop. I would be back in the so-called real world, a place that the corporate personnel types I encountered while attending the corporate training for Quality of Work Life had never experienced. Everything looked so clean and doable on paper, in a classroom, or in a seminar setting, but putting anything into action on the shop floor was altogether different and very challenging.

As mentioned earlier, the second shift began at 3:30 in the afternoon, but the supervisors came in thirty minutes or so earlier to walk the shop floor with their counterparts from the first shift to learn what the "hot" or rush items of the day were— basically finding out what was going on that day. I also found that, much like my situation in the personnel department, I had no place in the office to work from. No desk. No drawer. No place for anything. I know this is difficult to fathom, as General Motors was the world's largest and most admired automobile manufacturer at the time, but I had to resort to using a shoebox for my personal items, for department and plant notices, and so on.

The very first order of business to take care of was to have one of our fork truck drivers retrieve some tooling from our production storage area. I was very specific and detailed in what I asked the employee to bring up to the shop so I could assign it to one of our tradesmen. When he came back with the incorrect tooling, I just stood there and thought that nothing had changed since I'd left a year and a half before.

Once the day shift clocked out, Mac and I introduced each other to our new janitor, a member of the United Automobile Workers. This guy was something else; it really made me wonder how the auto industry and GM in particular had been as successful as they had been. By the end of the second day, we had not seen this guy in our department at all. Zilch. Nada. Zero!

Mac told me he would take care of the matter the following day. The next day he told me that he had made up his mind to write a grievance on this employee. To make a long story short, he was sucked in by this guy and let him off the hook. Well, how did that work out for us? This janitor spent most of the day in Medical because, as he told me, he hurt his back performing his job assignment. He had done absolutely nothing for three days. He was one of many employees that were protected by the UAW and their bargaining agreement with GM.

Fast-forward to Saturday of that first week, a time-and-a-half payday for the hourly employees. Who do you think showed up for work late, with a cane and sporting a doctor's slip? You guessed it, our "exploited" janitor. This guy did next to nothing on Monday, Tuesday, and Wednesday and was absent without calling on both Thursday and Friday. Meantime, our shop was taking a huge hit in the housekeeping area. So this day he strolled in, *even though he was not scheduled to work*, and expected to put in an overtime day.

Since I was running the shop alone that day, I decided I would confront this situation once and for all. Needles to say it was to be a very, very long workday, but at about 9:30 that evening it was all over.

The report below, requested by our Labor Relations Office and written by me, detailed the events of that Saturday, November

10, 1979, which turned out to be invaluable in the subsequent grievance procedures dealing with Mr. G as well as determining his future with the company.

Mr. G clocked in at 3:06 p.m. but he first reported to me at 3:45 p.m., cane in hand, limping, and sporting a doctor's excuse for his condition. I had him wait in the cafeteria while I decided whether I should put him to work or not.

At 4:12 p.m. I told him to report to the shop and at that time would inform him as to what he needed to do.

At 4:18 p.m. Mr. G was asked to come to the office, and I placed him "On Notice" as per Shop Rule 8. Then, out of the blue, he said to me, "You've been shot at before, Sarafin."

I told him, "One more threat, whether a witness is present or not, and I will call the police and have your ass taken out of here."

The question is this: "How did he know a shot was fired through the front window of my home more than a year ago when the first time I met Mr. G was this past Monday?"

He was given direct orders by me to change the towels and clean the wash basin, and sweep the floor in the men's room, and sweep the wood shop. Upon hearing this he asked for his union committeeman, and I told him I would do that, however, he was to begin his job assignments. He then asked for a Medical Pass, which I had to give him. At 4:24 p.m. he left the shop and went to see the nurse in our medical department.

At 4:29 p.m. I called the Medical Department and discussed Mr. G's problem. The nurse told me the following:

(1) He told her he was under mental stress.

(2) He told the nurse that I must be having marital problems.

(3) The nurse noticed an unfilled prescription dated 11/9/1979, and this day was the thirteenth.

Mr. G reported back to our department at 4:41 p.m.

At 4:57 p.m. I noticed Mr. G sitting on the toilet with the door open and still *nothing* had been done by him.

At 5:05 p.m. the UAW committeeman began talking to Mr. G in our office and at 5:14 p.m. he asked to see me in the office to discuss the situation. During this session, I asked Mr. G to read his doctor's excuse to me and the committeeman. I then asked him what his last day worked was. He did not reply. I told them that the excuse stated, "Reinjured back on 11/8/1979." I reminded him of the fact that the last day he worked was Wednesday, the seventh, and on that day with the plant nurse he stated he "hurt his back lifting a box." I told him there was confusion regarding the dates, and at that time his response was, "That's real good, Sarafin."

At 5:34 p.m. I terminated the meeting because I could see we were getting absolutely nowhere. The committeeman told me that the two of them would be going downstairs to file a grievance against me, at which time I reminded him that after a reasonable length of time Mr. G would be expected back to begin his job assignment. He responded by asking me if I was trying to tell him how to do his job; I simply restated my position.

At 6:09 p.m., Mr. G and now two union committeemen were still in the UAW union office, so I called them and told them that they did in fact have a reasonable amount of time to file the grievance and that I would be expecting Mr. G back on the job at 6:20 p.m.

At 7:00 p.m. I got a call from the day shift production superintendent, who was called at his home by the UAW union committeemen in regards to what was going on. They had an approximately forty-five minute conversation about the situation in the shop of which I was not privy to. The superintendent called and told me Mr. G would be back to the shop to do his assignments.

Finally, at 7:20 p.m., Mr. G and the two committeemen came into the shop and presented *me* with two grievances, which I signed. I then asked the janitor if he had his lunch as yet, and he replied that he did not. I told him he might as well take his lunch at 7:30 p.m. with our group and then get to work on his assignments. He replied, "Might as well." [Keep in mind that the janitor was to begin work at 3:30 p.m., and it would be 8:00 p.m. once lunch period was over, and he had not lifted a finger to help us out in the shop.] One of the committeemen said he hoped we would not have any further difficulty this night. I replied by saying, "I hope not."

Mr. G finally showed up after his lunch. However, it was 8:15 p.m., and when I asked him where he was the last fifteen minutes, he told me he took a break. I told him. "You don't take a break right after you have a lunch break." At this point I gave him a direct order to sweep the center area of the shop, where there was a lot of sand on the floor where production tooling had been dismantled. It was an obvious housekeeping situation and safety hazard as well. He told me he couldn't do the sweeping with his cane, so I told him to leave it in the office and it would be safe. He picked up the broom and walked slowly with a limp toward the office and placed the broom against the office wall and asked me for a Medical Pass, his second of the night, which I gave him.

While I was instructing him on the assignment, he asked me, "Why do you want to die?" I totally ignored him.

He returned from the Medical Department at 8:30 p.m., and at that time I asked him to have a seat in the office. At 8:40 p.m. I called the nurse and asked if there was anything else she could do for Mr. G. She told me she could not do anything for him and advised him to see his personal physician for his nervous condition.

At 8:45 p.m. the UAW committeeman was back in the shop office, and I told both him and the janitor that if he was not on his assignment by 9:00 p.m., he would be issued a pass to go home.

At 9:05 p.m. I issued Mr. G a Special Employee Pass for 9:12 p.m. in the presence of his committeeman. [Keep in mind that this guy was clocked in and getting paid from 3:15 p.m. and had not done anything in five hours.]

I was sitting in the office with our tooling change supervisor as the committeeman and the janitor were making their way out when all of a sudden the committeeman was pounding on the window yelling that Mr. G was hurt. I immediately called the nurse and grabbed a wall-mounted stretcher, and I had the other supervisor call for security.

Mr. G was crumpled on the ground with no blood visible and unresponsive, and by 9:20 p.m. he was strapped on the stretcher and being rolled out of the shop and taken to the local hospital by security.

Finally, after six hours of nonsense, the shop was quiet and in shock over what had taken place. I simply could not make up this kind of story. Once things settled down, I called the plant nurse and asked if there was anything unusual when she checked Mr. G while he lay on the floor. She said he had a completely normal blood pressure and heart rate in spite of all that was going on. He was, in my estimation, a real pro at working the system in order to get paid for doing nothing. The fact that anyone, including the union, would protect someone like this is why the labor movement has steadily eroded in this country.

I never heard what the outcome of this episode was, but I never ran into Mr. G in the plant again. Thankfully he never returned to our department, which was all right by me.

The following week went by very nicely, followed by a week off to hunt whitetail deer in the southern tier of New York State with my dad, brothers, and friends of ours as we had done for many years. Dad hunted with us through his mid-eighties until his emphysema would not allow him the luxury anymore.

On November 26, 1979, my first day back after a great week of hunting and camaraderie, I discovered soon after hitting the floor that our new milling machine from the Bridgeport Machine Tool Company was not yet operational. When I asked about the delay, I was told the maintenance department had assigned an extremely overweight electrician (we jokingly called them bulb changers) the week I was gone to wire the machine. The problem was that when one of our machinists went to turn it on, the motor took off in reverse and began smoking. I was told the electrician threw up his hands in defeat.

It should be pointed out that these electricians made very good money as skilled tradesmen, and as long as they were "good employees," this kind of thing had no consequence. The union protected them, and in a situation like this, their supervisor would send another electrician and hope for the best.

I also found out that our department brain trust was attempting to blame the manufacturer for shipping a faulty machine. It was difficult to think that they really believed that a company such as Bridgeport would deliver a piece of equipment without it being totally checked out. Of course, that would not happen.

The question was why our department or plant manager did not decide to spend the money to have the manufacturer set up the machine correctly from the start. We'd had it for a month and a half, and it was still not in operation. What a shame that a company such as General Motors acted so foolishly and by doing so did nothing to maintain the confidence of the tradesmen we supervised. Thankfully, the second electrician did know what to do, and we finally had our machine ready to be productive.

After a rather benign week in the shop, I was summoned to the salaried personnel director's office to go over my performance appraisal. This appraisal covered my year and a half working on special assignment as Quality of Work Life coordinator. Because of my less-than-professional experiences with reviews in my direct area, the shop, I was anxious and apprehensive about the process but looking forward to hearing his opinion.

When I arrived in his office, he was seated at his desk with a large folder in front of him. It was the appraisal package, and to my total surprise he took an hour and fifteen minutes going over his opinion of what I had accomplished and how I had handled all of the non-QWL duties. He rated my potential as "Eighth Level Short Range."

Let me explain the levels quickly for some perspective. A first-line supervisor, which was my position in the shop, was level 6. A general supervisor, one who oversees the first-line supervisors, was at level 7. He had my short-term potential at level 8, which would require leaving the model shop and moving onto the production floor as a production superintendent. This would be the only way for me to achieve that level, because the shop was a dead end in so many ways. Finally, he had my long-range potential as "Unclassified," which really blew me away, because in our plant of 2,500 people, only a handful of folks, the plant manager included, were at that level.

Needless to say, I was not only extremely pleased with his assessment of my performance but also grateful for the effort he put into my performance appraisal. I knew it could be quite beneficial for me in the near term. I appreciated it, and I told him so.

There is a saying in Buffalo: should you not like the weather, wait around for fifteen minutes and it will change. Well, the day after my appraisal, December 6, 1979, while I was still enjoying the good vibes brought about by my appraisal, one of our College Graduates in Training (CGIT) confided in me an incredible story involving him and another CGIT and a night-school class they were taking at Erie Community College (ECC). Both of these young men had the first-shift general production superintendent as their plant adviser.

They said their adviser asked them both to provide him

with a written critique of this special class they were attending at ECC. It appeared to be quite innocent, and they dutifully complied with the request and turned in their critiques. The trainee I talked to thought this was a means for their adviser to determine the appropriateness of the class for our business model.

To their amazement, they discovered that both of their critiques had been mailed to the ECC instructor by the adviser. Believing that their critiques were intended strictly for in-house purposes, they were understandably shocked and embarrassed when the instructor nonchalantly informed them of receiving copies of their critiques from their GM adviser. Even more stunning was the fact that the manager pulled this very unprofessional stunt while the young men were still taking the class. I cannot imagine how they must have felt.

The following day was very normal and quiet, but I must comment on what I heard during the week concerning our plant's cold-box core-making plans. Earlier in the book I explained that, in the casting process, a core generally formed the internal shape of the casting whereas the pattern or model formed the external shape. For example, the engine block on your car received its shape via a pattern or model, and the cylinders were formed by cores. Our cores were made of sand mixed with oils and cereal, and cured by baking in core ovens, or they were made of sand mixed with resins and cured by natural gas-heated tooling.

The powers that be were hell-bent on converting a large portion of our core making to the cold-box method, which mixed sand with resins of a different chemistry and passed a gas through the tooling and sand cores to cure them instantly.

The problem was, as I saw it, that by the time our casting plant began planning for this process change, we were already the last facility to do so. As a matter of fact, the General Motors plant in St. Catherine's, Ontario, was already returning to the hot-box method because of escalating chemical and catalyst costs. The other drawback was that this process had to be controlled more rigorously because the gasses were very harmful if inhaled; if not thoroughly exhausted, they also posed an explosion hazard.

The bottom line was that even though everyone knew of these things and the results at the other plant, it was full steam ahead on cold box. Only time would tell whether this decision was the correct one for our plant. It reminded me of the warnings of icebergs that were not headed by the captain of the Titanic.

This same week an incident of belt tightening took place that involved the steel crib, a caged and locked area on the production floor near the maintenance shop where all steel-bar stock and flat stock was stored and dispensed as requested. These raw materials were critical for plant operation. Until December 14, 1979, there had been a crib attendant assigned to dispense and log the materials provided to the skilled trades people for their work.

One of my guys came to me to inform me that he had gone to the steel crib to pull some cold-rolled steel for a repair on a piece of production pattern equipment only to find the steel crib locked, with no attendant in sight. He told me he heard that because of recent reduction of manpower in this area, one person was taking care of the steel crib as well as pumping gas at the oil house, which was outside of our manufacturing plant.

Since my curiosity got the best of me, I took a trip downstairs to see for myself what was going on. I ran into the crib attendant as he was returning and asked him why he wasn't at the steel crib when one of my guys needed some stock. His answer floored me and made me wonder how this plant could remain a viable concern. He told me that his orders were to drop everything and lock up the steel crib whenever he got a call from dispatch that someone required a fill-up for a plant vehicle such as a fork truck.

I asked myself, *Does having skilled tradesmen, who are making around twelve bucks an hour, standing around waiting for material save money?* Worse yet, not being able to complete a project could lead to production downtime or scrap. It didn't make any sense, and after all these years it still evades all logic. I guess it looked good on paper.

The next day I was in the production area and ran into the newest supervisor in the core department. This bright young man was a recent graduate of the General Motors Institute and excited about his supervisory position; he was very eager to contribute to the company's success. He told me of an incident that had taken place the previous week. I was floored by what he confided in me and also disappointed, especially after being the Quality of Work Life coordinator for our plant for a year and a half.

His story was brief: He was on vacation the previous week and had arrived back in town on Friday afternoon. Shortly after arriving home, he received a call from the plant telling him to report to work the next day, which was a Saturday and technically still his vacation period. I remember telling him how very sorry I was that his manager had done that to him and also that I was terribly disappointed to see that all my work with QWL had not penetrated the dictatorial environment of the organization. We had a long road ahead of us.

END-OF-YEAR HOLIDAY PLANT SHUTDOWN

I am not sure what year the practice began, but for many years our plant would completely shut down production for about two weeks spanning both the Christmas and New Year holiday season. Only certain maintenance people came in to do work that would be difficult if not impossible to do if the plant was in run mode. This holiday break was instituted because it was too difficult to operate the plant efficiently when you had absenteeism and drinking off the charts. Management felt it wasn't worth the fight, and the UAW used it as an opportunity to get *paid* time off for its members.

In 1979, December 20 and 21 were the last two days prior to the holiday break, and it was indeed an extraordinary experience. Everyone received two paychecks: second-shift people were paid on the twentieth and day shift and third shift were paid on the twenty-first. This resulted in a sort of carnival atmosphere, including drinking, dope, sex, gambling, and unfortunately a killing of a UAW secretary during a daylight robbery at the offsite office.

One incident involved a core room supervisor and one of his men. The supervisor had recently purchased a bar a couple of blocks from the plant, and for some time plant security had been doing surveillance on both of them and had them on film. This time they left the plant too early, for an excessive amount of time, and for the last time. They were fired.

Merry Christmas and a Happy New Year!
Bring on the '80s!

Chapter 11:
1980—TOUGH TIMES HIT GENERAL MOTORS

JANUARY 1980

A brand-new decade had begun for the world, our country, the General Motors Corporation, and the thousands of employees eager to meet the challenges that lay ahead for the US automobile industry. It was also the beginning of a new decade for our shop, and I was rested and prepared to contribute all I had to the success of the operation.

While off work for the nearly two-week holiday period, I drew up a communication regarding our upcoming implementation of the cold box process in the core room, which was going to be a huge and difficult undertaking. I had our secretary type it for me and sent it to the second-shift general superintendent of production, the person whose desk I had shared during my QWL tenure. I also copied the plant manager and the first-shift general superintendent of production.

My letter, dated January 7, 1980, had as its subject "Training & Education of Employees in the Cold Box Process" and read as follows:

> In the very near future the Metal Casting Plant will embark on a completely new process of core making; namely the "Cold Box Process." I believe that in order for this endeavor to be a success we must not limit our planning to the mechanical and process side of this project.

It is of utmost importance for us to begin planning for the education and training of our people because this is a totally new concept of core making as far as our Metal Casting Plant's personnel are concerned.

We must not leave any stone unturned in this most important step toward our development as a world class metal casting plant. Without good and positive education and training of both our salaried and hourly employees in regard to this cold box process there will be some exceedingly tough times ahead in our attempts to bring this endeavor to fruition.

During my tenure as Quality of Work Life Coordinator I was exposed to a number of excellent training programs which were utilized by various GM and Chevrolet Plants in order to make their new production processes successful; and successful they were. Our own Tonawanda Motor Plant, for example, developed an excellent program which involved the training of both hourly and salaried personnel prior to the V6-60 Degree Engine startup. This was not a panacea as they still had problems, however I am sure that they were much fewer than if their plans did not include the education and training of their personnel.

Their training of hourly and salaried personnel had another very important benefit in that all of the people who were involved worked more closely together when production began. A better situation rather than the almost constant you this, me that attitude which only becomes worse and not better.

I suggest that our Management Group take a look at how the Tonawanda Motor Plant's training was structured as this could act as an excellent thought starter for a program of our own which would address our cold box changeover.

Generally, this education and training should consist of the following:

1) Off site training of both hourly and salaried personnel covering: a) safety, b) tooling, c) machinery design and operation, d) materials involved, e) explanation of total process, and f) explanation and description of cores AND castings involved.

All of the following should be accompanied by detailed visual aids to promote learning and to maintain a high level of interest. Models of cores and patterns would be an invaluable tool for our personnel to gain familiarity with our products.

2) In-plant training of hourly and salaried personnel including the following: a) Master Mechanic Department tour with explanation of the castings, core tooling, and process, b) informational tour of the Core Department addition from top to bottom, c) hands-on training of ALL processes and on ALL equipment, and finally d) gaining a rapport between the Core and Molding Departments. These employees should be assembled at least once so they can become familiar with each other and with each other's product.

To insure the continued success of our plant we must have all of our departments working as a team.

What I have offered is a general outline and suggestions for a training program however in my current position in the Master Mechanic Department I am not involved in the developments concerning the cold box process. However, given the opportunity I would love to help in any way to make this project a success.

It is my opinion that a Secondary Cold Box Committee should be developed consisting of representatives from all disciplines and both Unions (UAW and Patternmakers League). This could be the current Hot Box Committee but would also include a more thorough cold box penetration into our management group.

These suggestions, which I believe would have created a much-improved system changeover, were not even discussed with me, let alone acted on. No one in management thought to approach me about the letter, not even to say thanks for the effort. I had seen firsthand the difficulties involving tooling differences and the issues with the pipefitter, electrician, and machine maintenance disciplines in understanding the more demanding system, which could have been alleviated with a strategic roll-out of this particular cold box process.

This was the first time that I felt the year and a half of effort being the Quality of Work Life coordinator for our plant had been in vain, as our management philosophy remained status quo, at least for the time being.

On January 8, 1980, as I walked through the shop at the start of the second shift, every one of my people that I encountered asked me the same question: whether the rumor that twenty-seven patternmakers were to be laid off soon had any merit. I had to tell them the truth: I did not know anything except what Mac, the general supervisor on day shift, had been telling his people that this was coming down. He did this kind of thing all the time. These situations seemed to give him a feeling of superiority and of being in the know. As a manager, he should have known that always bleeding bad news on the rank and file has a negative effect on morale and therefore productivity. It simply was not called for then or at any time in our shop or the plant in general. I told my guys that I would advise them of any concrete information that came along.

The next day I ran across a situation that was very similar to the cost-cutting measures involving the steel crib. This time it was our department's tool and supply crib. I was told that we were completely out of two sizes of hex head nuts. I did some investigating, only to discover that the purchase requisition for those items was still on our department head's desk, waiting for his signature. Then they had the nerve to ask why a piece of tooling wasn't ready for production. In addition, and as a result of the skyrocketing price of silver, we had to resort to locking up our silver solder, as it had become a highly desired material for thievery.

Unbelievably, this wasn't the end of the ridiculous goings-on that day. The next incident involved a three-drawer file cabinet. As per an "approved contractual demand," the company was to provide a three-drawer file cabinet for the shop committeemen. However, because our plant manager had issued a "furniture moratorium," any requisitions for furniture required his signature. It made you think about why Chevrolet paid all their department supervision so well while not allowing them to make even rudimentary decisions like this one. The file cabinet was eventually provided as per the union contract.

On January 10, 1980, one of the many rumors making its way through our shop came to fruition, and it was a real shocker even though the writing had been on the wall for some time. Our department head notified the union committeemen of the Patternmakers League of North America that fourteen patternmakers were to be laid off as well as 175 production workers and thirty-five maintenance men. The effective date was to be January 18, 1980.

We were all told that the reason for the cuts was that production of V8 cylinder cases (blocks) was being dropped from 1,600 per day to 1,100 per day. That was a 31 percent drop of the most profitable job in the plant. Coupled with this was the loss of the companion castings, such as the cylinder heads, for the V8 engine.

I thought it would have made sense to wait until the start of their last week to make the announcement, because I and the other supervisors had to attempt to maintain an effective and safe shop for a week, knowing fourteen of us would be hitting the streets.

In retrospect, the guys in our shop who were the first casualties were the fortunate ones, as some of them ended up with opportunities in the adjacent motor and forge plants, and one or two relocated outside New York State.

Yes, these cuts were made because of the reduction of the volume of castings, but they were made across the board, affecting not only production people but the service departments too. It did not mean that electricians would have fewer problems to address or that the maintenance department would all of a sudden have 30 percent fewer machine breakdowns. And in our department, the production tooling service crew would actually have more work because of shorter runs, requiring more frequent changes on the production lines. Unfortunately all of these service departments would have to do more with less, and I worried about the safety implications of all of this.

That January was like no other that I had experienced in the plant since being hired sixteen years before. Each and every day that I walked into the shop, my stomach tightened with tension as I anticipated what may have come down earlier in the day. This day was no different. A week before I had left a message for our assistant department head about when our first-line supervisor shift rotation schedule would be determined and posted. I mentioned in the message that I had asked the department head about it, but he had directed me "down" to him. I emphasized in the note that it wasn't so much the shift that was important as when we would be working them, because we had personal lives and families to consider. The question in my mind was why a simple decision could not be made in less than a couple of weeks. My God, any decision would be better than none at all.

Upon arriving at the shop on January 14, 1980, I had just removed my coat when the assistant department head informed me that I would be in Detroit all of the following week, attending a "train-the-trainer" workshop for an upcoming in-plant, seventh-level supervisory program that must have been mandated by corporate. It was not hard to tell that he was not very happy about it, but it was out of his hands. He told me that I would be joined by a member of the plant staff, the head of the materials department for our plant—a real nice guy.

This assignment came as a complete surprise to me, and it had to be the plant manager who decided that I should do it, possibly because of my experience with presenting the QWL seminars. When I went downstairs to get some detail about it, I learned that the plant manager had directed the staff member I was attending with to drive to Detroit over the weekend rather than take a flight. It would be a five- to six-hour drive, and the program would begin at 9:00 a.m. sharp on Monday. I wondered how General Motors could be so broke that it couldn't afford plane tickets for us. And, to put the icing on the cake, we would not be compensated for the time driving up and back from the event.

Even as the times were demanding that everyone come together for the cause, the following three days proved that ego, status, jealousy, and a me, me, me attitude was so ingrained in the culture of GM ,including our plant, that I doubted anything would ever change.

Our plant was the only General Motors plant casting a V6 ninety-degree case and cylinder heads, primarily because our guys in the "wood shop" developed that V6 by removing the rear two cylinders from the popular V8 model. This six-cylinder engine was the forerunner to the sixty-degree V6, which would be mounted transversely to accommodate front-wheel-drive vehicles.

This incident involved tooling that made a core that formed the exterior of the top of the cylinder head for the V6 engine. We were in the process of adding some casting thickness in an area requiring welding, machining, and final bench work. The evening prior, I left a note for the day shift in our log book, asking them to check an area that I believed was finished off improperly. It simply did not match the corrected epoxy model of the area in question. Someone had accidentally removed excess material where it should not have been removed, and I was simply doing my job to point it out. If left alone, it would result in a thin area in the casting, which it could have been a very costly oversight resulting in scrap castings and failures in the field. What took place next was not a complete surprise to me, but it was remarkable in light of the challenges our department and the plant were facing.

The following day, prior to the start of my shift and while being taken through the shop, both the day shift supervisor and general supervisor told me that the areas of minimal metal thickness "were not important" regarding the work done on the tooling the previous day. I could not believe they uttered those words. I thought it was much too serious an issue to have pride enter into the decision-making process. After all, anyone is allowed an error here and there, so why try to cover it up?

The next day, January 17, 1980, my general supervisor informed me that the tooling in question—the same tooling that a day earlier had a problem that was said to be unimportant—had been thrown in the trash. Well, that was one way to end the discussion: simply throw away tooling worth twenty thousand dollar without a shred of paperwork—none, zero, nada! This absolutely did not have to be done, as it could have been repaired simply by adding a little weld and reshaping the area. I truly believe that this went down as it did because I was the supervisor who caught *their* error, and they could not live with it.

January 1980 was turning out to be one of the most difficult periods not only for the casting plant as a whole but for our shop as well. Friday the eighteenth turned out to be a new life experience for me as a person and as a supervisor. It was the last day for fourteen of our skilled patternmakers, who were being laid off indefinitely due to slumping car sales and the resulting lowering of production schedules. I couldn't help but think how fortunate I was to never have been let go like that.

The men involved were noticeably shaken that day. Midway through the shift, one of them came to me very upset and asked if he could leave early. He simply could not stay the full day. Since he was not in a good place mentally, I issued him a pass to leave early. Before the shift was over, I shook each man's hand and wish him the best, while painting as optimistic a picture as I could. I believe they all knew it had been a great run while it lasted. I thanked God when that workday was finally over.

The months of February and March of 1980 went by smoothly compared to January, and even though that was a welcome relief. I had the sense that more grief would be coming down the pike.

APRIL 1980

Even though the arrival of April was very welcome, it did not mean that spring had arrived in Buffalo. But anything would be better than the long, dreary winter season we had just endured.

April was also the month that one of our veteran supervisors returned to work after having been on sick leave because of abdominal surgery complicated by a heart attack during his recovery. This guy was fifty-eight and had thirty-eight years with General Motors. I assumed he was in pretty good shape financially. The two numbers, fifty-eight and thirty-eight, when added together gave him ninety-six points, which was significant at the time. (The General Motors retirement age [eighty-five points] was calculated by adding years of service to your age.) This supervisor could have retired with full benefits five years earlier at fifty-three, but he had decided to continue to work.

I had a difficult time understanding why, considering his physical condition, he did not see fit to retire and spend some quality time with his wife and family. I was told that he was overheard saying that he would receive improved benefits if something happened to him while at work. I thought that to be a ridiculous way of looking at his situation and life in general.

He returned to the job with stipulations, playing the system to the hilt, with one of his restrictions being that he was not to work any overtime because of his physical condition. What burned me was when he was on the day shift (seven to three) he would have 10:00 a.m. doctor appointments, and when he was on night shift (3:30 p.m. to 11:30 p.m.), his appointments just happened to be in the late afternoon. Management did not address this, even though it was obvious he was gaming the system.

One evening he told a couple of us during break that he had blacked out behind the wheel of his car on the way to work. Fortunately, it was just for a split second, so he was able to recover and bring the vehicle under control. How he passed the plant reentry physical after his last medical leave was beyond me.

A few days later I spotted him walking across the top of very large production tooling in our storage area and immediately told him to get the hell down before he had a bad accident. It would be bad enough to simply fall, but to land on steel vent pins that were tapered and about eight to ten inches long would not be a pretty sight.

About the same time another supervisor, who was sixty-four, came back from triple bypass surgery and was merely going through the motions and not being much help in running the shop. However, he must have been feeling quite well at home, because he had been cutting tree branches on his property when a branch hit the ladder. He fell about twenty feet and landed on his shoulder; he was fortunate that he was not killed. He spent several days in intensive care, eventually recovered, and retired. Smart man!

MAY 1980

Even with all that had been going on in the plant and with General Motors over the past year, I didn't begin feeling a nervousness in my gut until May of 1980. I couldn't get the shop out of my mind—not even at home—for fear of what might have happened earlier in the day.

Then on May 8, 1980, the plant began offering all salaried personnel fifty-five years and up early retirement. I knew right then and there that the game had changed from a little belt tightening to something much more serious. This was being done because of the continuing poor market conditions and in anticipation of impending salaried employee cuts. To my surprise, word had it that not many of those fifty-five and older had agreed to the offer, although there was one supervisor in manufacturing who at forty-seven and twenty years of service had elected to take it.

Because of the low initial response to the program, rumor had it that the age requirement might be lowered to fifty-two. I joked about whether my thirty-seven years would be too young for the early retirement option.

Keep in mind that while all this drama was going on, the first-line supervisors had to maintain calm in the ranks, because we still had tooling to take care of to ensure that the plant had proper tooling to maintain its schedules. This was not an easy task for any supervisor, including me.

Immediately upon arriving in the shop the following day, the tooling change supervisor and I were asked to see the department head in his office. All I could think was, *What now?* He asked us to take a seat, and proceeded to inform us of what was going on with the business environment and with future layoffs at the plant and our shop. In the fifteen minutes he had us in his office, he did not give us any numbers for the plant or for our department, and most importantly he did not divulge who might be affected in our department. So, why did he bring us into his office and put on a show like he was keeping us in the loop when he told us zero?

After the meeting, my colleague went down to the production floor to get his men on track for the day. When he returned to our department, he told us that thirty salaried employees would be axed, and he had six names to boot. He had garnered the information from a production superintendent, who told him that our department head surely had the same information. We had a saying in the shop: you want to get answers? Ask the janitor.

Earlier in the book I wrote about the fact that our production clerks had suffered cutbacks, and when I kiddingly asked a female clerk about all the overtime money she was earning, she gave me a look of disgust. It was 7:00 p.m. when I talked to her that evening, though she was officially attached to the third shift, which began at 10:30 p.m. She told me she was working the three and a half hours gratis, with no overtime pay. I thought it ironic that the plant would pay a janitor to come in for a sleep on overtime, but for a valuable person, such as this clerk, it was no dice.

It's important to make the distinction here that the janitor was a member of the UAW, whereas the clerk was on her own as a salaried employee. For many years, I worked "on the bench" with union representation, but in a supervisory position, I didn't have representation. And I could see the pros and cons from both sides. I thought that one day the whole salaried workforce at General Motors would be "unionized." Many decades have gone by, and it has not even come close to that.

On May 12, 1980, the personnel department conducted meetings most of the day to inform the salaried group of the "tough times ahead." They attempted, but failed, to assure us that no one would get screwed; that all layoffs would be done as justly as possible and would be announced on May 15. I wondered where all this was heading. Although we all knew the automobile business was in a funk, it was still unimaginable to think our plant would be closed, especially when you took into account all the money that had been poured into the plant recently. So we went back to the floor to run the shop while attempting to put the fifteenth out of our minds.

The next day, our second-shift production superintendent held informational meetings of his own for the salaried folks under his command. This was the manager whose desk I'd shared while I was the QWL coordinator. He was a great, smart, personable man, and on this evening he painted a grim picture for the plant. He explained that the people who would be getting released had not been told yet because Central Office had not given its blessing to our plant's requests. He also hit on something not brought up at the personnel department meetings: we were being hurt not only by Japan's auto invasion but also by our neighboring plants in Canada. All the news during those times was bad news, so everyone was on edge in the plant.

The entry in my notebook on the May 15, 1980, was "What a massacre." Of the thirty employees who were notified that May 30 would be their last day, many had been General Motors employees for many years. The following day we found out that our entire supervisory group had dodged pink slips, but several had to drop back a level. This meant they would have the same responsibilities but a smaller paycheck.

Another item of note at this time had to do with the casting plant's bid for the four-cylinder engine program (cylinder block and head), which was vital for us to remain a viable casting facility. First we were told by upper management that we had lost our bid, which was a terrible blow to our plant's future. Then they told us that we were once again in the running because the planners discovered a four-million-dollar transportation advantage due to the proximity of our plant to the motor plant where the castings would be machined and assembled.

Did they expect us to believe that GM's planners and managers did not realize, after twenty-five years of operation, that our plant was only a fork truck drive from the motor plant? Not many of us did, and if it was true, it's no wonder GM was losing money. My opinion was that it was all scare tactics, but to what end? As it turned out, our plant never did get to produce the four-cylinder castings, and the bad news kept piling on.

JUNE 1980

Although June of 1980 was pretty much business as usual, a letter distributed by our plant manager reinforced the desperate atmosphere in our plant and in the US auto industry in general. In this letter to all salaried employees, he stated, "These conditions have resulted in a net loss for the second quarter of 1980 which more than offset a marginally profitable first quarter. Thus for the first time since the depression of the 1930s, GM reported a loss in a quarter not impacted by a major strike." He went on to say merit increases for all salaried employees worldwide would be suspended, effective immediately.

Just to be clear, suspending merit activity meant a pay freeze, but how could one explain why salaried pay freezes had not taken place after the many strikes by the union? My opinion was that neither union strikes nor economic conditions were the fault of the salaried workforce, so why should the plant manager or the corporation use these conditions as an excuse to freeze pay?

Then he implored us to "redouble our efforts" when we were already doing much more to cover for the men and women who had been terminated.

The other point to make here is that we had zero control

over the design or pricing of the product and that the Japanese manufacturers were delivering vehicles with an improvement here or there at a price that was highly competitive. The bottom line, as I saw it, was that it did not matter how hard we worked at the plant level; unless the corporate mindset and product design went through some major improvements, we would continue to experience a reduced market share.

Other than that, the month of June was quiet, but on the last day of the month, which happened to be my first day covering for the vacationing pattern (tooling) service supervisor, the guys in the crew (UAW hourly) told me that our plant manager had stopped all in-plant retirement dinners because of the plant's belt tightening. This was just another example of people on the floor knowing things before many of us supervisors.

At times like this I felt embarrassed being a part of the great General Motors Corporation. No matter the situation, it was shameful that a heavy manufacturing facility could not afford a five- or six-dollar dinner in the plant cafeteria in appreciation of those employees having twenty-five or thirty years of service? In my opinion, that stunk to high heaven.

JULY 1980

On July 19, after checking the department log book, I donned my hard hat and ear plugs and headed to the production floor to begin another day. I quickly learned that one of my guys had a court appointment, and with one already on vacation, that left me with only five men to accommodate the entire core department and seven molding lines in the foundry. This manpower situation presented a challenge, given the fact that before initial plant layoffs, this crew on day shift had thirteen men.

Some of the equipment changes required three men, and there were lunch and break times to consider. It was just nuts, and it posed a safety issue with guys running from job to job and rushing around. I am talking about removing and installing large tooling on rather dangerous equipment, which required following safety procedures fully to prevent serious bodily injury or worse.

At about eight that morning, my department head asked me how it was going. I thought, *Is this a trick question?* Anyone who knew anything about what these guys did, and especially a department manager, would know that it would be challenging for sure. I told him exactly how it was. His response was to ask if the employee who had the court date would be coming in later. I couldn't believe it, and after a few seconds of silence I told him that I doubted he'd return. What did he think would be the consequences of cutting this crew by almost 50 percent?

Two days later, these employees called their union committeeman to lodge a formal complaint about the amount of work assigned and the related safety-related issues. They did approach me to say that their grievance was not against me personally, because they knew that I did not control the numbers of employees. I appreciated that.

When I finally made it back to our shop, my three superiors were sitting in the office not really understanding, or caring, how hellish it was down there on a hot July day with all that had to be done with such limited resources. Once I had their attention, I said that five men should not be expected to handle the entire core and molding production. Amazingly, they sat there with no reply, though at other meetings they had the gall to talk about morale, commitment, and loyalty and all the other catchphrases. Where was their commitment to their subordinates when it really counted?

Near the end of the month an accident we had reminded me of a story my dad had told me years earlier about one at the DuPont chemical plant where he worked for thirty-five years until his retirement. He told me that someone had placed a broken broom handle in a trash barrel with the jagged, broken end standing up. When the janitor went to grab the liner to empty the barrel, the broken handle poked his eye. Fortunately the man did not lose his vision. When their safety engineers attempted to reenact the accident to verify the injured man's story, the safety supervisor came close to poking out his own eye. Luckily the damaged broom handle tapped his eyebrow, which made him a believer, I guess.

At the end of the month of July, I heard that an electrician had received some minor burns when an electrical panel box exploded and blew the door off. For some time, the on/off switch on that panel had not been working, forcing electricians to use the main breaker for the on/off function. During the investigation of the accident, two supervisors, who apparently were not convinced by the injured man's story, decided to reset the door, turn on the power, and pull the breaker as the injured man described. You guessed it; he pulled the breaker and the thing blew again. Fortunately, no one was burned, but one did get foreign bodies in his eye.

I just had to tell my dad what had happened at my plant. I reminded him of the story he'd told me many years back, and I had to come clean and tell him that I had found his story a little hard to believe at the time. We had another beer.

AUGUST 1980

Early in August, we heard that our plant was "awarded" the casting for the new four-cylinder case, but it was only to make up for what the Saginaw plant could not produce. It was good news for a change, but it would not hit our plant for at least two years, and anything could happen during that time.

Toward the end of the rather quiet August at the plant, we heard that we would be losing one of the bright young men who graduated from the General Motors Institute with an engineering degree. This guy worked his way through the ranks and eventually served as a superintendent of production in all of the departments in the plant. He was a sharp guy that everyone liked and would be missed by GM. We heard he was going to a casting plant in Pennsylvania for more salary and a better position, possibly as plant manager, as the current manager was to be retiring soon.

The investment in dollars into this young man had to have been astronomical, yet the General Motors Corporation, and in particular our plant, didn't seem to give a damn that talented folks such as he were leaving GM for positions which offered some upward mobility. You had to wonder who would be the next employee to hitch his wagon and leave or be let go.

The last Friday of the month had me as the lone supervisor not only overseeing the model shop but also the tooling service guys in the production area. It came as no surprise to me that rank would be pulled on this last shift prior to the Labor Day holiday. I was always good enough to handle these situations, but they would point to my year and a half on special assignment as QWL coordinator and use it as an excuse about me not being up to speed on my performance reviews.

To top things off, our department head told the union committeeman that fifteen of our men would be laid off the next week without breathing a word of it to me. You would think he would inform me first rather than have me hear it from the union. Great Labor Day news, huh? Have a nice holiday.

SEPTEMBER 1980

This would turn out to be a particularly difficult month. It began with a meeting of supervision with our department head for the purpose of bringing us up to speed on short-range department projects and so on. The last two items covered were the upcoming layoffs *and* telling us about a special project for the V6 ninety-degree block. We had been told that this V6 project "would probably preclude any layoffs in our department." When I heard this, I just couldn't understand why he would have told the union about laying off people prior to a holiday weekend when it was not a sure thing.

The very next day we were told that five of our guys with up to twelve years' seniority would be laid off that week. I found this to be very difficult to deal with, because I'd worked with these guys prior to entering supervision and in some cases knew their families. What would they do? There simply were no other employment opportunities for their specific trade outside of the automobile business in Buffalo, besides the fact that the economy was tanking. It would surely be tough on them.

In the middle of the month, I had heard from good sources on the production floor that a very popular production superintendent and long-time employee threatened to go back to an hourly position if the constant interference from upper management persisted. He was referring to the plant manager and the general production superintendent, and that was bold stuff. I had never heard of anything like it since being hired in 1964. Things were getting testy for sure.

The plant also learned of another experienced employee that would be leaving at the end of the month. This salaried employee's wife had been laid off recently, and he had been cut back from general supervisor in the inspection department. When I caught up to him, he told me he had just about all he could take of the place. He added that the headhunters he talked to told him they were having a field day with General Motors salaried employees who were either laid off or had simply become disenchanted with the conditions. This demand, however, would not last indefinitely.

Then on September 26, 1980, we were informed that the corporation gave us the go-ahead to cast one thousand V8 engine blocks per day. This was very good news—the best we had heard in some time. However, the powers that be still hadn't decided on what production line these castings would run, and that was huge for our department. The downside of this good news was being told that none of the laid-off model makers would be called back, even though there were a hundred pieces of equipment that needed to be made ready for whatever line they would eventually run on.

There had been a pattern of reduced production requirements with subsequent layoffs and then increased production numbers without any rehiring. I knew this could only go on for so long, and then what?

OCTOBER 1980

It was the sixth of October when we found out that the production numbers for the V8 engine blocks, which had been 500 per day and then 1,000 per day, were increased to 1,600 per day. However there would be no rehiring, including the tooling service people, who were running from one assignment to the next with barely enough time to get their tools in order for the next assignment. Neither I nor others in supervision could understand what upper management's plan was, and it made us all a little suspicious as to what was going on behind closed doors.

One thing I can say about my days at the casting plant was that there was never a dull moment. On October 7, 1980, our wonderful maintenance department was spraying part of the exterior of our plant with some type of green enamel paint. At the end of my shift, I went to the parking lot to my new 1980 Chevette. I was shocked to see and feel green specks all over the hood and roof of the vehicle. One of my fellow supervisors told me his vehicle had the same damage. You may have guessed it: it was paint overspray that had been spread throughout the parking lot by a nice Buffalo breeze. There was no telling how many vehicles were damaged, and the subsequent bill to the plant would be high. Someone would be on the hot seat, for sure.

About eight days later I talked to the personnel director about this issue, and he told me that 150 were involved and the owners would be notified about how to proceed with the repairs. The plant dodged a big one in that most of the vehicles were able to be repaired by buffing the affected surfaces. My vehicle was as good as new.

On October 17, 1980, because of my involvement in the salaried United Way campaign while QWL coordinator, I attended a luncheon in the plant's salaried dining room. The purpose was to thank all of those who were solicitors for the campaign. My new department head, who was also the chairman of the drive, did a commendable job of thanking those who made it a success.

However, two things bothered me about that event. My first beef was that the general production superintendent, who was the plant manager's representative, never said a word—not even a thank-you. Fortunately, the maintenance superintendent caught the inappropriateness of this and stood up to thank the chairman and all involved. After the meeting I thanked him for his comments.

The second bothersome point was when we had some hourly employees retiring, the plant couldn't afford a lunch in the cafeteria for them, but somehow this luncheon was justified. I didn't get it and was not at all comfortable with this kind of behavior. But you just had to keep on truckin'.

Five days later, we had sixteen men in our shop receive their 25 Year Service Award; they had their choice of a watch or a clock. However, the awards presentation was not held in the conference room downstairs but in our small supervisors' office. To make things worse, the general supervisor—not our department head—did the honors. No fanfare. No lunch. I thought, *How cheap and unprofessional to handle it this way.* And the whole spectacle was witnessed by most of the model shop guys, as our offices were exposed because of their glass fronts. Not a good feeling.

Later our department head posted a directive on our departments' bulletin board stating that management expected supervision to stick to the policy when running the department and asked the employees for their cooperation. On October 20, 1980, on day shift, one of my employees returned to work after an "unexcused" day off. That was his twenty-fifth day of absence for the year. About an hour or so into the shift, I called him to the office and presented him with the balance of the day plus one day off as the penalty for his behavior. Though he was miffed, I felt that his penalty was way too little and much too late. After all, with a month of unexcused absences, the only penalty was a day and a half off without pay. That was not a deterrent. At times like that, I felt the union was doing more harm than good in that it was protecting nonperformers while the plant was struggling to remain viable.

The very next morning, the third-shift supervisor asked me for my opinion on his not penalizing an employee, who was an alcoholic, for surpassing the unexcused absence limit. His reasoning was that this was his first violation since coming to the third shift. I told him that I did not agree with him; I didn't want to be the only supervisor adhering to policy.

Later that morning, I asked to talk to our department head about this issue. I explained to him that I didn't want to be the only supervisor going by our policies. I got nowhere with him, as he simply said, "We have a policy, so let's follow it." Incidents like that made me want to pull my hair out; they were so discouraging.

The October 1980 door could not be closed without one final kick in the stomach to me and my colleagues in the model shop as well as other departments such as electrical and pipe fitting. On October 24, our general supervisor told us to perform safety inspections of all the chains for the overhead hoists in our department. We were like, *What?* Never in my sixteen years in the plant did anyone other than a safety supervisor or safety engineer do this task. It was the safety department's responsibility. We simply were not trained to do it.

One would have to ask the question "If they weren't going to do this, what was it that they were being paid for?" Also, if I or the other supervisors were doing lift hoist inspections, we couldn't be there for the skilled men we were supposed to be supervising. And what about the enormous liability for us should an employee be injured? In the end, we had to do it and to put our signature on each and every overhead hoist in the shop. The union committeemen filed complaints because they too were uncomfortable with us performing a safety department function. All I can recall is that it was a one-time event.

The skilled trades have lines of demarcation. For example, a mechanic might have to stop a job because an electrical device needs to be removed before the job can proceed. Union lines of demarcation could get ridiculous. In the chain inspection fiasco we, as unrepresented employees, had to do what management said or could be shown the door. In many instances, and in its purest sense, the union acts as a check and balance between union employees and management so that shortcuts are not taken that could have catastrophic consequences. That is a good thing.

NOVEMBER 1980

For me, November always meant that it was time to go whitetail deer hunting with my dad, brothers, and friends. This was no secret at my workplace. The season's opening day was November 17, and on the fourth my management team had not given me their blessing to go or made sure my position was covered. I had discussed this with my general supervisor and asked for that week off months in advance, but this guy was incapable of making decisions, especially concerning personnel matters.

I should mention that I was the only person on our management team who took a week off to hunt. This so-called general supervisor, who was earning forty thousand a year, pushed the decision onto one of his pets, who since the cutbacks was at supervisor level like I was. It would be like you making a decision involving one of your coworkers. It was absurd, but I eventually prevailed and was granted the week off.

At the end of our shift on November 6th, the second-shift tooling change supervisor came to the model shop office after starting his men downstairs. With the supervisors from both shifts all gathered in our small office, he asked my forklift driver,if he had fallen over the lumber that was on the first floor waiting to be brought up. That was his sarcastic way of saying, were you too busy all day to bring it up, without knowing what went on the previous eight hours. Everyone in the office heard what he said, however my driver merely gave him a dumb sort of look without a comment, which was not totally unexpected from this guy. He simply walked out of the office.

Incredibly, as if on cue, my general supervisor asked me where the lumber was, knowing full well that it could only be in one place. I looked him directly in the eye and told him, "Outside the elevator door on the first floor, where it has been all day." I could see he was taking the side of his favorite supervisor on the second shift, but he dropped it there.

The following day, the same second-shift supervisor (Mr. Perfect who was always complaining about having too much to do) asked our tooling change supervisor the same question about the lumber as the day before even though he and his driver did not touch the wood delivery either.

All involved in this episode would have to be deaf and blind not to have known that I had been working all week with two of my men clearing out and cleaning forty feet of storage racks used to keep our many fixtures. I went home all week black like a coal miner from scrapping two gondolas of old, outdated, and obsolete equipment so we could enjoy room to store our fixtures rather than throwing them all over the place. I took on this project on my own, and management totally ignored it. There were no rewards or thanks beyond payday, at least in that department.

I had known for some time that if I were to have any chance of advancing in General Motors it would not be in the model shop but in manufacturing and possibly another plant altogether. It was also a no-brainer that I would have to do some self-promotion before the QWL coordinator glow was forgotten history. With that in mind, on the November 11, a week prior to my vacation week for hunting, I paid a visit to our plant manager to discuss my desire for upward mobility within the corporation. I told him that I believed I could gain valuable insight from his experiences while working his way from a supervisory position all the way up to plant manager. Bold would be an understatement.

The plant manager did not give any immediate suggestions; he was courteous and positive while being noncommittal and illusive. However, I don't feel it hurt the cause to let him know face to face that I had the desire and ambition to do more in the General Motors Corporation.

DECEMBER 1980

December was always a short month because of the extended plant shutdown that usually began on the day before Christmas Eve and ended on the second day of January, assuming it didn't fall on a weekend. The third-shift melting department would come in on the evening prior to the first shift on January 2 to begin the massive undertaking of awakening the sleeping giant. This startup of the cupola melting system was big-time manufacturing and nothing to take lightly, as molten cast iron needed to be ready for the first shift, when the plant began pounding out molds.

On one disastrous day during the week prior to the holiday, our plant ran damn near 100 percent scrap on all the molding lines due to a high sulfur condition in the cast iron. This metallurgical mishap resulted in castings that were extremely brittle. It was first noticed in the cleaning room, where castings were literally cracking while they were moving along the conveyor system. Some of the larger castings actually split in half. It was a nightmare for sure and certainly not what a struggling plant needed at the close of the year.

The irony in this was that the second-shift general production superintendent, the person who had befriended me during QWL, was a graduate in metallurgy from Mellon University and extremely knowledgeable in the field. A year earlier he had spent a week in the Saginaw casting plant studying their melt lab. We did not have a melt lab and had to take iron samples to the lab in the forge plant for testing. It was a slow and arduous system, and it had finally caught up to our plant and cost us big-time. The purpose of his trip then was to gain some insight into how they were process testing their iron. With that information he put together a plan for a dedicated melt lab at our casting plant.

As usual, the bottom line was that there was zero money for this project, which meant we had to continue to use the forge plant's lab next door. Unfortunately, it bit us on the behind this time.

Our shop had its own aha moment that December month when our brain trust finally realized that the new cold-box equipment, which was to hit our shop within days, would weigh eight thousand pounds all booked up. "Booked up" meant the complete tooling set consisting of the lower half of the tooling affixed to the transfer car and ejection pin assembly, the cover half of the tooling, and the blow plate, through which the sand mixture was delivered under high air pressure into the core cavity, producing the core.

This was a huge problem for our model makers, because they would assemble these tooling sets, check clearances, and so on, as they did for all other equipment, and those would either be moved to storage or sent directly to the production floor. The problem was that our hoist rails were not rated for that kind of weight, and the air hoists themselves were barely safe for the weight.

We didn't have to look further than our own department to find this kind of management failure. First, the pattern design department should have told our managers about this. No one up front should have slipped up on this critical detail, considering the chosen few had gone on junkets to the job shop in Michigan where the tooling was being built. The purpose of these trips, after all, was to make sure there would be no surprises. That was wishful thinking.

On December 17 th, which our last day prior to the long Christmas holiday shutdown, I was leaving the plant and walking through the exit tunnel (necessary because of the train tracks that ran alongside and between the plant and our huge parking lot) at the end of the first shift. I happened to find myself walking alongside the general supervisor and second man in charge of my department. There was not much conversation, but about halfway through the tunnel, he nonchalantly said, "You'll be going to second shift after the holidays." He looked at me as if he was looking for some kind of approval or something.

This absolutely floored me; I think I even staggered a bit. I thought, *Wouldn't the office have been a more appropriate setting for this announcement?* My goodness, what would he have done if he hadn't run into me in the tunnel? The possibilities would be mind-numbing.

Soon 1980 would be history, and I could only hope that somehow, some way 1981 would bring improvement not only to our plant but also to the General Motors Corporation and the US economy. I could not see any hope if we were to endure another year like the one we had just experienced.

Chapter 12:

1981—THE UNTHINKABLE BECOMES REALITY

January 5, 1981, was the first day back to work after a very nice and long Christmas holiday spent with my wonderful wife and our two great daughters as well as family and friends. I had tried not to think about my job and just wanted to recharge my batteries for what I believed would be a pivotal year not only for the plant but also for me personally. In early February I would be beginning my eighteenth year at the Tonawanda Metal Casting Plant, and it was very difficult for me to fathom that after seventeen years of service there was so much uncertainty about my future as well as the future of the plant.

It was not only the first day back from the holiday but also my first day back to the second shift after eight months on day shift. It was like walking into a morgue as we only had two machine operators for the eleven machines in our shop and had only about twenty or so model makers working on the bench. It did not take long for discouragement to begin to seep in.

It also did not take long for me to hear all about the terrible plant startup we had endured that morning. Buffalo is usually pretty damn cold in January. And with all of the heat being shut off to save money over the holiday shutdown, everything froze. For the first crews to come in, it was like walking into a freezer locker. The maintenance crews were overwhelmed with cracked pipes and valves throughout the plant. This resulted in many large water leaks throughout the plant including our department. In addition to this, the first-shift production molding lines could not begin making molds, because there was no molten iron available until well into that shift. Many people had predicted bad things were to come of plant managements' austerity plan and they did.

I had to give our second-shift general production superintendent credit because he had pleaded for the heat to be left on. But no one listened, including the plant manager and his management team. As I said, this was done to save energy costs, but I could not even attempt to guess what it cost the plant in repair and parts, lost production, and employee morale.

This brutal and disappointing first day back at the plant reinforced my resolve to give it one more year for something positive to develop with my career, or I would be moving on.

During this rough period in our plant's history, with layoffs of both hourly and salaried folks, and battling high scrap rates and multiple changeovers to accommodate shorter production runs, it was not uncommon to have a person in management try to do things to bring positive attention to himself or herself, thereby hoping to stay away from a demotion or, even worse, the chopping block.

One such case took place on January 21 and involved a core room superintendent and me. This production superintendent called me at 7:25 in the evening and told me to change the foundry schedule from a passenger-vehicle cylinder-head casting to a marine intake manifold casting for the next morning's production run. I am sure there must have been a pause on my end of the line, because on so many levels this was nuts.

First, the production planning office called in all of the schedules to our department for tooling changes at 2:00 p.m., and from that point on the wheels were in motion to do just that, both in our shop and on the production floor, for the following morning. In addition to this, all the people involved in that decision had gone home for the day—at 3:30 or 4:30 in the afternoon. This particular production superintendent should have left with them, because I believe at the time he was suffering from battle fatigue. He had gotten to the plant by 5:30 that morning, so that means he already had fifteen hours in that environment. That was nuts, and so was he.

I decided that I was not going to go along with his request, even though I was certainly outranked. After much discussion and my willingness to explain what he should have known, he rescinded his request.

This situation would have turned out very badly for this guy because cores were already in the pipeline on the overhead delivery system, and a change to the marine casting would have meant losing at least forty-five minutes of production while making the adjustments the following morning. He would have been in hot water and would have had to do much explaining to the brass the following day. Even though I saved this guy's ass, he didn't have the class to ever tell me thank you. How was that for quality of work life?

January 23, 1981, was the last work day for my most fervent supporter at the plant, and though I was happy for him, it was a sad day for me. He was the general manufacturing superintendent who allowed me to use his office and desk and who recently had pushed my resume on to a couple of plants to see if any positions were available in manufacturing. His new position was as the director of metallurgy for the Buick Division in Flint. This was a huge promotion, to say the least, as well as a huge loss for our plant.

Though he was an excellent manager, knew metallurgy inside and out, and was a great guy, it was somewhat surprising that anyone at the plant was moved up, especially someone like him. He was vocal toward the plant manager in expressing opinions when it came to the melting department as well as his disagreement with plant management regarding the heat-on or heat-off fiasco over the holiday shutdown.

I went to his office as soon as I heard the news and could break away from my department to congratulate him. He was beaming, as I believed he knew he could not remain at this plant for career reasons, and he would be leaving a casting plant with a bleak-looking future.

Right out of the blue he told me that as a result of his sending my resume to the motor plant, I would be receiving a call for an interview within a couple of weeks for a general supervisor position or better. He knew damn well my career would be stymied in this casting plant, and he told me just that. I thanked him for moving my resume to the proper people, wished him all the best, and never saw him again.

Sadly the phone call never materialized, and I never found out why I was not contacted for the interview.

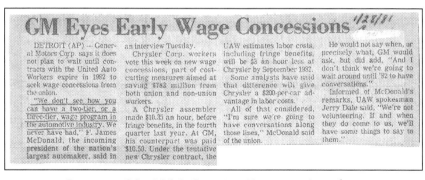

January 28, 1981 Courier Express Article –
GM Eyes Early Wage Concessions.

The article above, which was in the January 28, 1981, issue of the now defunct *Buffalo Courier-Express*, talked about the fact that the General Motors Corporation did not want to wait until the United Auto Workers contract expired in 1982 to seek wage concessions from the union. The company wanted to get this done as soon as possible, but I and everyone I talked to believed it would not fly. And in the final analysis, it did not.

General Motors could not just send down a communiqué and show a movie and cut wages like they did with the salaried workforce, freezing wages and cutting rank in June of 1980. The UAW would not hear of that, period, and it never happened.

I found it interesting how our plant complex in Tonawanda and the General Motors Corporation in general made astronomical amounts of money for thirty years, and after one bad year, the corporation was singing the blues. I and most employees understood profit and loss, stock price, board of directors, and all of that. But why couldn't they make some sound decisions to make us and the corporation successful, like having better design and better mileage?

Not two days later, one of our maintenance department supervisors stopped by our office to chat for a few minutes and told us an interesting story. He said that because of a poor tool crib inventory as well as poor tool quality, one of his mechanics actually clocked out of work and bought, with his own money, a twenty-eight-dollar tool so he could complete a repair assignment. I know this is hard to believe, but again, you can't make this stuff up.

FEBRUARY 1981

One day the safety engineers walked through our shop and directed our department to remove the buckets that we had strategically hanging from pipes and other things to catch water leaking from the ceiling. Management told us to comply with the request.

Since our shop was on the second floor with a flat roof that had been poorly maintained over the years, our ceiling leaked when it rained or when snow buildup began melting. This had always been an issue in our department, with all its negative effects on our machines and the model makers' expensive personal tools, which were sensitive to moisture. Our men hung the buckets as a preventive measure, because GM was not willing to maintain the building and, God forbid, cut into profits.

At the start of my shift on February 9, 1981, a severe water leak was evident above one of our craftsmen's work areas. I decided to pay a visit to my department head to tell him that without the buckets and without the roof being repaired, it was not a good situation to work in. He simply told me to "go out there and hang a pail back up there."

This was a GM executive decision for you: violate what the safety engineer had just told us just days earlier. I guess he figured that was the path of least ramification; that way he wouldn't have to call the plant manager to ask for a new roof, a request that would have been rejected anyway. This was the way things were in General Motors, at least at this plant at that point in time.

A couple of days later, on February 11, 1981, I attended a showing of the corporation's *Outlook '81* film, which would be viewed by all hourly and salaried employees in General Motors Corporation. The message of this film was about where the corporation was headed and generally what its employees were expected to do to get there. It obviously was, and had to be, a very general view because of the diversity of operations and facilities. It certainly did not address any of the problems of manufacturing centers, such as at the casting plant.

I assumed that corporate management expected and trusted that upper management of these plants would implement plans and programs that would be consistent with their *Outlook '81* vision. That was a huge assumption, to say the least, because once the dog-and-pony shows left town, it was business as usual. It was like the Quality of Work Life process, which went full bore when I was the coordinator, but then faded into the background, and the plant continued to struggle with its top-down management style.

A very interesting thing took place after the film wrapped up. Our plant manager talked to the assembly and said that our supervision team was doing a fine job. Then he said the recent heavy production schedules of the Mark IV engine (a large V8) were due to the heavy scrap rate in our plant. However, one of my brothers, who was employed at the motor plant then, told me that they were "running the Marks out," which meant we were losing another product line to another facility. So much for being honest with the employees.

One thing the plant manager told the gathering that wasn't a lie was that twenty-eight salaried employees would be laid off very soon. How's that for an outlook for the year 1981?!

A week had gone by since the *Outlook '81* meetings, and I was beginning to get a little concerned that I hadn't heard from anyone at the motor plant regarding either my resume being sent over in early January for review or for an interview for any open positions at that plant. I decided to take the rather bold step of calling the plant manager. He and I were members of the same local country club, and we would say hello when we happened to see each other, so it was not a cold call. I told him that I would really appreciate a chance to interview with the motor plant for a supervisory position in manufacturing. After a brief discussion, he set up an appointment to see me two days later, on February 20.

On that day I had my meeting with the plant manager of the motor plant, I was confident that my work, school, and special assignment history would put me in a very good position to be considered for an opportunity there. However, as he explained to me, his plant was experiencing its own difficulties; they were actually doing some cutting. But he did tell me he would get his personnel director to talk to me.

I left the meeting confident that I could not be shot down

because of my employment history or character, but in the end I was never contacted by the personnel director or anyone in his department, and I never called to find out why. I felt like this was just one more nail in the coffin as far as my career advancement in General Motors.

On the same day, a letter written by Robert D. Lund, then general manager of Chevrolet Motor Division in Warren, Michigan, was distributed to salaried employees. The letter, dated February 20, 1981, announced that Chevrolet and General Motors (in that order) were to engage in a major activity called "Let's Get America Rolling." It sounded to me like another act of desperation over the poor economic environment our plant and the corporation were experiencing.

The letter began with this salutation: "Dear General Motors Alumnus." I wondered, *Why did he distribute this letter to us? We are still employed by GM. Does this mean we will soon be joining the ranks of past employees.*

Maybe he should have had his letter proofread, because "Let's Get America Rolling" actually was a two-phase program, one for retail cash bonuses and one for GM salaried retirees. Maybe they thought that once we completed a grueling shift, we could call all our friends and relatives and ask them to buy a Chevrolet to stimulate the economy.

More importantly, the folks I knew in the plant, including me, were not looking to make such a substantial purchase as a new automobile in the midst of all the layoffs, both past and announced. Added to this was the uncertainty about the economy during that time and about the direction our plant was heading.

Finally, to call this incentive program a "major activity" was amusing; this was the kind of junk we had come to expect from GM corporate. How was this going to contribute to our facility becoming competitive in this very competitive and mature business? The short answer was that it would not have any effect on our daily struggle.

He concluded his letter with "We at Chevrolet are dedicated to being the catalyst for the economic recovery that we know is absolutely essential." Upon reading this statement I had to ask myself what could he be referring to. With all of the salary restructuring, layoffs, increased workloads, and at our plant the curtailment of the Quality of Work Life process, one would have to question how this would be a catalyst for anything but more grief.

On a lighter note, a funny episode took place during the workday on March 11, 1981, when our model shop group attended a Cancer Screening Preview Session, which was presented by our plant personnel director and a General Motors corporate medical doctor. Each of us was to endure a colonoscopy because employees in our trade across all plants exhibited a higher incidence of colon cancer than employees outside our trade as well as the general public. One of the probable reasons for this was because of all the dust we inhaled while cutting and drilling the asbestos board used for heat barriers in our hot box core tooling.

To familiarize us with the screening process, a sigmoid scope was passed around so we could understand how the exam would be done. During this familiarization process, one of the guys noticed the instrument was made in Japan, and when he asked the doctor if the scope was made in the USA, there was not much of an answer. However, the point had been made: buy American.

The next day, March 12, 1981, rumors were going around the plant that our newly assigned production superintendent would be the one from our plant joining a group of managers traveling to Japan for a two-week tour of casting facilities. General Motors Corporation was very good at spending money on programs like this that would not help us out of the critical position our plant and the company found themselves in.

To me, this was like putting the cart before the horse. What I mean by this was described in an article in the March 1981 issue of *Modern Casting* magazine. It made the point that the Japanese manufacturers had superior housekeeping, three-hour inventories, truck drivers assigned not to one but three fork trucks for casting delivery, and around-the-clock, seven-day (two on, two off) operations. None of these practices could have been employed at GM or our plant because of the labor agreements with the United Auto Workers.

At our plant we found it difficult to keep sand and water off the production floor and aisles, and we had twenty-five trucks waiting to be repaired with only two mechanics on the entire second shift to work on them. We hadn't come to grips and conquered these rudimentary challenges, let alone the more complicated ones.

It didn't make a difference to me who was selected to participate in this charade, but the production superintendent chosen from our plant had just been reassigned to production from his former position of superintendent of plant engineering. I felt that, rather than wasting two weeks in Japan, he would have benefited much more from an intensive training in foundry practices so he could recognize what he would be looking at when decisions had to be made on the manufacturing floor.

I knew that American companies and GM in particular, would not get anywhere as long as supervisors did not have any clout and as long as performance depended on how the employee felt, we could just forget quality and productivity.

At a salaried meeting on March 15, 1981, the Japan trip and the manager chosen to take part were officially announced. He then solicited ideas and suggestions that he could take with him on the trip. As usual the room went quiet, and the meeting was adjourned.

My brief note to him, below, which I gave to him on March 17, 1981, was one of the very few, if any, responses.

To: Mr. J. M. Richards, General Prod. Manager

From: Jim Sarafin, Supv. Master Mechanic

Date: 3/17/1981

I am writing you at this time in response to your in-plant correspondence dated March 10, 1981, concerning the Japanese foundry industry and its workforce.

First of all, if you have not had the opportunity to see the article on Japanese foundries in the March 1981 issue of *Modern Casting* magazine, I have enclosed a copy for you, and I hope it will be of some help.

Secondly, all I hear about in regards to the Japanese foundries is productivity, robotics, new techniques, quality circles (which to some degree I implemented in our plant through QWL), and employee morale. I have not heard nor have I read anything about how they deal with their non-performers, hourly and salaried alike, which I have to believe they must have. I seem to doubt that they offer life employment for the non-performers? I'd really like to know what their attitude is in this regard.

Another question I have is whether the Japanese managers feel that stable employment is the key to the high level of morale, loyalty, quality, and productivity.

Last but not least is the area of skilled trades which I feel we both are very interested in. Specifically, how do they deal with the skilled people in terms of productivity, teamwork and morale?

I want to thank you for the opportunity to have some input into your upcoming experience and will appreciate hearing from you in this regard.

Sincerely,
Jim Sarafin

Of course, when he returned from the two-week Japan tour I didn't received any acknowledgement from him that he received my input, and aside from delivering a report on his trip through a series of salaried employee meetings, I did not receive any correspondence about the questions I forwarded in the memo, and they were not addressed in his report on what he had learned in Japan. I felt I had wasted my time on that one, but I was not at all shocked by it either. It was the GM way.

Here is my last diary entry for March 17:

> I've been on the second shift now for almost three months and can honestly say that, conservatively speaking, I have spent 30% of my time doing hourly employee functions consisting mostly of material and tooling handling. I am quite confident that this is not what GM is paying me for.

Because our crews were cut to the bone, there would be no way for them to meet production schedules without my assistance. It was really a shame.

GM to Widen White-Collar Cuts

3/30/81

Associated Press

DETROIT — General Motors Corp. will eliminate up to 27,000 white-collar jobs over a period of months in the second such action in a year, the Detroit News reported today.

The newspaper quoted unidentified company officials as saying the reductions would eliminate between 8 and 15 percent of GM's salaried work force of 180,000.

The officials said, however, that the cuts more likely would affect 13 percent of the salaried workers — even to the level of company vice presidents.

Reductions would come through closing some departments, consolidating others and not replacing some workers when they retire, company spokesmen said.

In an interview with the De-troit News, GM Chairman Roger B. Smith said the reductions would be handled delicately and over a period of months, removing only non-essential positions.

"We're not going in with an ax," Mr. Smith said. "We're using a surgeon's knife."

The automaker announced last April that it intended to trim its white-collar work force by 10 percent, or 19,000 people. That across-the-board staff reduction resulted in 10,000 employees actually leaving the company.

The first indication of more staff cuts came several weeks ago, when about 600 of GM's top managers were told to review all the functions within their jurisdiction and consider what ones could be eliminated.

March 30, 1981 newspaper article – GM to Widen White-Collar Cuts.

The newspaper article above, out of Detroit and printed in the *Buffalo Courier-Express*, is an interview with Roger B. Smith, General Motors Corporation chairman, that was tough to read and was just another obvious sign that this thing was going to get very bad for a lot of employees and their families. As described, this would be the second such action announced since the beginning of the year and would impact up to 27,000 additional salaried employees.

When articles like this one came out, the question was how a supervisor was supposed to maintain high morale while also

143

maintaining the morale of those he or she supervised. It also was somewhat amusing how Mr. Smith used the terms "nonessential positions," "delicately," and "we're using a surgeon's knife" when describing the elimination of those positions. This "non-essential position" statement was baloney. Did he want everyone reading the article to believe that GM would be paying tens of thousands of employees for non-essential work? That was absurd because the employees, especially the salaried folks, surviving the cuts would be doing the work of two or three people while they were seeing their benefits and compensation reduced.

APRIL 1981

I was on vacation the third week of April, and I spent an awful night with a terribly upset stomach due to some bad mushrooms my wife had used in making mushroom soup. I still kid her about trying to get rid of me, because she did not get ill.

On the morning of April 16, 1981, I realized I was not and would not be in any condition to make my appointment at 7:45 p.m. with the plant doctor for the colonoscopy exam mentioned earlier. I immediately called the medical department in the plant around mid-morning and talked to one of the day-shift nurses about my condition.

Before I could complete my explanation, she cut me off and said, "I don't take care of scheduling for the cancer screening exams." I told her I understood that, but all she had to do was inform whoever happened to be in charge that I would not be able to make it. I felt like that should have done it, but I was wrong again to assume there would be any cooperation around that place.

At about 6:45 that evening, my general supervisor called me at home and asked if I would be coming in for the exam. He told me that the doctor and his corporate staff were done with the others and were waiting on me. I was stunned by this and was still suffering the effects of mild food poisoning, and I had to explain the whole situation to him.

If you happened to discuss the state of the economy and of our plant with plant nurses, they would tell you that they had the most difficult job in the place. However, they were merely pill pushers, blood pressure and body temperature takers. And if I had anything to do with it, that particular nurse would be dismissed, and she could go find work in a hospital. Then she would find out what work really was.

I found it amazing that I didn't even have to be at work for these ridiculous kinds of incidents to take place.

April 20, 1981, was an ominous prelude to some very bad times approaching for many employees of the plants throughout General Motors Corporation. An envelope was distributed to all salaried employees that contained a letter from our plant manager, introducing a letter from Mr. Stephen Fuller, vice president of personnel administration and development, discussing the "MODIFICATIONS to be followed in the ADMINISTRATION OF FUTURE SALARY WORK FORCE REDUCTIONS."

In the second paragraph of the plant manager's letter, he wrote, "The new procedures emphasize the importance of *employee's performance* and *contributions* when personnel decisions are considered." I actually felt good reading this because of my performance in the model shop, the fact that I had earned my college degree while working there, and the fact that I had been the Quality of Work Life coordinator of our plant for a year and a half. However, if past experience was any indication of what might eventually take place, I knew I had to look at this statement as a PR gesture to cover their butts in the carnage to come.

In the third paragraph of our plant manager's letter, he wrote, "Currently, a careful evaluation is being made regarding our total salaried work force in relationship to production schedules, sales and future programs. Every effort will be made to keep our anticipated work force reductions to a minimum; but, consistent with the requirements of our business."

In the end, all the references to performance, merit, and so on succumbed, at least to some degree, to plant and individual department politics.

The first sentence of the second paragraph said, "In 1980, General Motors experienced its first net loss since 1921—a loss which amounted to the staggering sum of $762.5 million." He went on to blame the "current business climate" and the "intense worldwide competition." Of course, he would not place any of the blame on not investing during all those profitable years in improved product design, performance, and aesthetics or in improved plant technologies (especially at our casting plant). All the while General Motors was succumbing to the United Auto Workers, primarily in the area of work rules regarding lines of demarcation that were very disruptive in the managing of maintenance at production facilities.

General Motors Corporation was in the process of spending some 40,000,000,000 dollars—yes, 40 billion dollars—in the five years from 1980 through 1984 to enable the "development of new products and technology, and obtain new plants and equipment." Nothing was said about investing in GM's employees; instead, two pages of the three page letter dealt with how salaried employees would be terminated, fired, "separated," or forced into early retirement.

I thought watching this scenario unfold in our department was going to be very interesting, and I wondered how I would fare in the eyes of my direct bosses and those of the plant staff who had given me the opportunity to demonstrate my abilities beyond skilled trades as QWL coordinator. Statements such as "emphasis must and will be given to the recognition of each employee based upon his or her individual performance," though sounding good, did not instill a great degree of confidence that it would work in practice. Politics always had a way of trumping the best of intentions or rhetoric in GM.

A few days had gone by since the unveiling of the new rules of engagement, if you will, when on April 23, 1981, I had an appointment with the personnel director of the GM motor plant, which was next door to my plant. This was acutely important in light of the dismal atmosphere in my plant, which did not look as though it would improve any time soon. I was very excited to have the opportunity to state my case as to what I could bring to the table as a member of their management team.

I thought that I handled my end of the interview quite well, and toward the conclusion of our meeting, the personnel director and two very influential people had spoken for me: the plant manager of the motor plant and the new director of metallurgy at Buick in Flint, whom I had come to know well while QWL coordinator. We discussed the possibility of relocating to another plant and looking in another geographical area, along with the possibility of my transfer to the forge plant. I felt that my background would be best suited for that plant, and if I were a betting man, I would have bet that was where an opportunity would present itself.

MAY 1981

The first day of May had me dealing with one of my "stars," whose job was to truck equipment as needed and to do general maintenance work on basic tooling as required. It was one of the best nonskilled positions in the plant. Right off the bat, I presented this guy with a penalty notice for a previous unexcused absence. Unbelievably, later in the workday, he was caught being out of the plant for between an hour and a half and two hours prior to his thirty-minute lunch period.

I had been suspecting him of this practice for some time, and on that day I had plant security call me when he left and again when he returned. I also had them hold him there upon his return until I could get to the plant entrance.

You may be thinking, *How could an employee simply walk out of a manufacturing plant at any time?* Because back in the day, just about all the employees who were not attached to a production line could slip out on break, lunch, or between maintenance jobs. They might go to the local pub for a cool one and wait to be contacted by the dispatcher via the two-way radios they carried—plant-issued, of course.

Once plant security gave me the documented times that he had been out of the plant, we walked back my office in the model shop, where I explained to the employee how easy it was for me to catch him violating work rules. He was not at all concerned about his situation, and he went on and on about how I was able to get into supervision and the QWL coordinator assignment because I played golf with management. Now, even if that were true, what did it have to do with his predicament? Nothing. The fact was that I did play golf in the Salaried Golf League, but only *after* I was promoted into supervision.

This illustrates one of the bad elements of unions, and in this case the UAW. Individuals such as this guy knew the "book"(UAW contract language) better than most supervisors and took advantage of the many disciplinary steps required. They played the game right up to the point where it would actually cost them. Then when contract time came along, all of these characters would get negotiated clean sheets so they could start all over in the penalty process. It was a terrible way to run a business.

I issued him disciplinary paperwork, including loss of pay for the time out of the plant, and that was that. He walked out like it was all a game, because he knew the union would eventually have his record expunged and he could start all over with his reluctance to play within the work rules. We as supervisors were being handcuffed with having to deal with this kind of employee, the unions, and management operating procedures while being expected by our bosses to maintain order and productivity in our departments. It was very difficult, to say the least.

On May 5, 1981, salaried supervisory employees were presented with yet another program spelled out in a document titled "Attachment; Information for Supervisors," which outlined "Changes in Employee Compensation Program." Interestingly, the last section of this program announcement stated, "Effective May 1, 1981, all classified employees in the United States and Canada will be encompassed by a single salary structure." It would have been nice to hear about it prior to it being enacted, but that was the GM way. At least at our plant it was.

The point should be made here that during this period of difficult times for General Motors, all of the wage revisions, salary structures, shift changes, firings, and so on applied to the folks that gave their blood sweat and tears for the company: the salaried supervisors and managers. This period was eerily similar to what we have recently witnessed in the federal government's auto manufacturers bailouts, where salaried employees and stockholders take it in the gut while United Auto Workers members continue on and have their pension funds and medical coverage shored up with taxpayer funds. And because GM had such a "good year" in 2011, employees received at least seven thousand dollars in bonuses, even though General Motors still owes somewhere in the vicinity of 46 billion dollars to the taxpayers of this great country. So, the question is, where is the bonus to the American taxpayer?

The main agenda point for this meeting read, "A 19-minute videotape which highlights the changes that take GM's compensation program for classified employees out of the 40's and into the 80's." Were we to believe there were no changes in GM compensation guidelines for forty years, or were they preparing us for really bad times ahead?

The crux of the new Employee Compensation Program

for supervisors reduced salary ranges from 180 to 22 which amounted to having more employees in fewer compensation ranges. In the master mechanic department, this meant that the "all-merit pay increases" for the poorest-performing supervisor to the best performing was 3 percent to 3.5 percent which was "similar to the 1975 guidelines." There simply was going to be zero incentive to be outstanding and to do the uncomfortable things necessary to manage an effective department when the upside would be only a half percent more in your paycheck.

Under "Current salaries will not be affected," it was explained that "actual salaries will *not* be reduced…. However, the *employee's salary will be frozen for a time* until competitive trends warrant increasing the maximum of the range." Did that mean no pay increases for two years or five years? And how long would the wages remain frozen?

Chapter 13:
SITUATION TERMINAL

JUNE 1981

It was June 1, and I was back on the day shift due to our first-line supervisor shift rotations. Normally this would have been a nice change for the summer months, but with the angst permeating the entire plant, it was not business as usual. The tension was so thick you could cut it with a knife. Before the end of my first week, word was out that there were to be more hourly and salaried layoffs and that management was already asking all salaried people fifty-five and older to consider early retirement. We were quickly slipping into the abyss.

On June 9, 1981, Mr. McKee, GM vice president of manufacturing, was visiting our plant and was to tour the manufacturing areas as well as the skilled trades departments, all of which had been spit polished to make a favorable impression. Of course our competitors, the Japanese automakers, had their facilities in this state of cleanliness 24/7, according to the managers that made the trip there. We simply did it for the dog-and-pony shows for the visiting brass.

In preparation for his visit, all supervisors were given a three-by-five cheat card that contained Quality Level Comparisons between 1980 and May 1981 year to date (YTD). This was so we could answer intelligently if Mr. McKee asked any question regarding the plant's performance. Utter nonsense. And he never made it up to our department. Amazingly, later in the afternoon, our department head came out and told us, "Mr. McKee was impressed with the condition of the plant and that the plant was performing very well." That was ludicrous, especially with scrap rates of up to 27.87 percent for castings we had been producing for years. I thought, *either I'm an idiot, or they are out of their minds.*

A brief summary of the 1981 YTD casting quality average scrap numbers from January to the end of May will illustrate what I mean: engine blocks, 13.2 percent; cylinder heads, 18.7 percent; inlet manifolds, 14.3 percent; exhaust manifolds, bearing caps, and brake drums (simple castings), 6.5 percent. That was a lot of scrap!

To top off the day, it was announced that production of the four-cylinder was being cut from 3,200 per day to 1,600. All was *not* well at the Tonawanda Metal Casting Plant, and everyone knew it.

In the next couple of days, a good thing happened to me: I was informed that I was to receive the full 3.5 percent merit pay increase. But a week later all supervisors were told that they would be responsible for having their white shirts and shop jackets cleaned. There were no such changes for the UAW, the electrical and pipefitting union members, or the production workers, because they were protected by their labor agreements.

It was also announced in that two day period during this second week of June that a new four-cylinder head casting committed to our plant had been postponed until January of 1982. Making things worse was the fact that the metal production patterns were already being made in a Detroit job shop and, at this point, might never be used. To top things off, the head of the industrial engineering department turned in his resignation after almost eighteen years of service to General Motors. He walked away to take a position with a small firm in Michigan. Just about every day, during this period, we would hear of another employee resigning or being included in yet another wave of furloughs.

Friday, June 19, 1981, was going very well when our assistant department head—the one I discussed earlier as having no desire to address personnel issues—approached me on the shop floor to tell me there was a conflict with my upcoming vacation the week of July 13; my general supervisor had put in for vacation time the same week. He told me to "work it out with him." This was crap, because I had put in for that week in our vacation book way back in early April so I would be able to play in the New York State Amateur Golf qualifying tournament. There was no conflict then, but now, all of a sudden, there was.

Once I explained what I had planned and that all the fees and club dues were paid for, he relented. I played quite well that Monday but missed going to the match play portion by one shot, which was a disappointment. You know the quote: Don't quit your day job!

On June 23, 1981, the supervisory group in our department was informed that 128 hourly employees would be laid off on Friday of that week and our plant would be running only three production lines out of eight. Not only was this disastrous, rumor had it that twenty-one additional salaried employees were going to be "separated."

JULY 1981

My one-week vacation made for a fast-moving month. However, that did not diminish the reality of the continued deterioration of our plant—the bread and butter of many families. On Friday, July 3, 1981, it was announced that the staff was to meet the following day—*July 4th*—to decide the next salaried employee reductions in anticipation of a one-shift operation. The result of this staff meeting would result in the layoffs of three hundred hourly employees as well as twenty-five to thirty salaried people.

This was staggering, because many of us remembered working thirteen days straight with one day off, only to do it all over again for most of the 1970s. In fact, while I was still an hourly employee, I came in maybe an hour late on a couple of Saturdays for the second shift and was be greeted by the assistant department head saying, "Good afternoon, part-time worker." Ludicrous.

On July 15, 1981, a two-page letter from our plant manager was distributed to all salaried employees. I do not recall if it was provided to all of the hourly employees, but I'm certain that the union brass received a copy.

The first sentence of his communication read as follows: "I am writing to you because I feel our jobs are being threatened by a Japanese manager we don't even know in a plant and country we have never seen." My response to that: "being threatened by a Japanese manager we don't know" was really about being threatened by GM's corporate managers settling destructive labor agreements simply to get manufacturing back up so their domestic competitors—Ford and Chrysler—did not pull customers from GM products. The United Auto Workers was smart in this regard, because it would choose to negotiate or strike the company that was doing the best in the marketplace, and in those days GM was usually it.

In that same sentence, he added, "…in a country we have never seen." This was troublesome because just three paragraphs later he went on to say, "Mr. Joseph Richards, General Superintendent of Production, talked about his two-week tour of 10 Japanese foundries." As the reader may recall, GM's managers saw firsthand exactly how they were beating us.

Why hadn't GM invested in its plants, technology, and employees while business was booming, and why was it not anticipating the market shift to lighter aluminum castings and plastic parts. Instead, one day it woke up and all of a sudden realized that the casting plant, which made GM a ton of money over the years, was outdated and not worth future investment.

In addition, bringing up items including "Absenteeism," "Outdated Agreements," "Wage Structures," and "Housekeeping With Out Janitors" had everything to do with the labor agreements that were negotiated between the United Auto Workers and General Motors. That, it turned out, would be difficult if not impossible to correct, because once work rules and lines of demarcation are established, it is very difficult, if not impossible, to take them back. However, there was absolutely no blame directed toward General Motors' corporate managers or plant management in general.

Near the conclusion of the letter was this: "There will be a reduction of both hourly and salary employees between July 24 and September 1, totaling 250-300 jobs. This is directly caused by all of the mentioned facts plus current schedule reductions, shutdowns and low sales."

Then, unbelievably, in his closing statement, he implored us to "join in a concerted effort to secure the future of our families and the retirement dreams of everyone." How lame and insensitive, when earlier in the letter it was shown that GM already had 80,000 to 100,000 employees unemployed and now hundreds and soon to be thousands of folks in the plant could see their futures going up in smoke.

Was there anything that anyone or any group could do to save the casting plant from total collapse and closure? I and all of the hard-working employees would soon find out the answer.

AUGUST 1981

On Monday, August 3, we returned from a weeklong plant shutdown—an annual event when large maintenance items were addressed—and came in early at 6:30 a.m. for a meeting called by our department superintendent.

The meeting covered new plant policies that, in a nutshell, would place many management responsibilities in the laps of the first-line supervisors, such as me. However, we could only operate within the UAW work rules, regardless of what the plant staff wanted. The agenda set for the meeting made it astonishingly clear that the supervisors were expected to cure all the ills of his department and of the plant, including housekeeping, safety, quality, cost control, and attendance.

With the recent push of the "We Team" propaganda, it was unfathomable to me that the plant staff would not have met with representatives of the UAW and the Patternmakers League of North America prior to having us, the lowly supervisors go on the shop floor and try to implement the changes, salvage any remaining moral, and try to get the work out. They were difficult days.

In summary, supervisors at the meeting were told they would be "responsible for cleaning their individual areas and equipment," "to inspect areas and equipment at the end of his shift," "to provide access to housekeeping equipment," and last but not least "garbage barrels and butt cans are the responsibility of the supervisor of that area." Management's theme was "no garbage or butts on the floor or in the parking lot."

Finally in section 5, "Attendance": "Each supervisor will be responsible for absenteeism." This was nuts! All a supervisor could do was write up the violation. Beyond that it went to Labor Relations and the union reps, period.

Many times during my employment at GM, when experiencing situations like this, I thought, *how in the world did a vehicle ever roll off a production line?*

Two days later, I found out that even though our plant had gone through its weeklong shut down for repairs, our shop elevator had not been addressed. It was out of order again because our department superintendent had not wanted to spend money for an outside firm to come in, even though this elevator was the only means to get the heavy tooling down to the manufacturing floor and back up to our shop.

On August 5, I was presented with the attendance aspect of the new policies. The actual IBM card from that day, below, shows four men on vacation, two men absent, one out sick, and four requesting early quits. That made eleven folks out of 35, or 31 percent of my shift, out all or part of the day. However there was nothing I could do about it because of past labor agreements negotiated over the years between General Motors and the UAW and the Patternmakers League of North America.

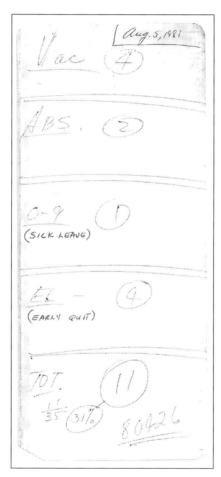

August 5, 1981 note card.

The landscape was changing rapidly, and on a Tuesday, August 11, another announcement was made that 155 hourly workers would be laid off, including seven skilled trades' guys from our department. This involved guys in my department with sixteen years of seniority; this was not a good situation for me. Even though I had more than seventeen years there, my time in management did not count as seniority in the shop. This meant that if, or more likely when, I was separated, I would not be going back to the hourly group but out the door.

The following day, there were meetings all afternoon in our department, with the result being that the second shift would be dissolved. The first shift would be from 7:30 a.m. to 4:00 p.m. with the third shift running 11:00 p.m. to 7:30 a.m. Everyone knew that this would create chaos in the melting department, because having to fire up the cupola furnaces daily was a disaster waiting to happen. In addition, the third-shift employees, upon their arrival to the plant, would find the plant blacked out to save utility money.

On more than one occasion, the plant manager was seen going through the manufacturing floor pulling electrical breakers just to make a point. This was a stupid and very unsafe act on his part, because having maintenance personnel in the bowels of a piece of large equipment during a loss of power could be disastrous.

Things were so bad during the last ten days or so that general supervisors were doing maintenance work just to keep the place going, and more salaried layoffs were scattered across the plant. In fact, one supervisor with thirty years of service was separated, which meant no health care or full pension benefits. These scenarios, which were taking place regularly throughout General Motors, resulted in countless families being hurt terribly.

SEPTEMBER 1981

Tuesday, September 2, 1981, turned out to be a very bad day for Jim Sarafin. I was told that I would be separated on September 30, 1981.

Those two sentences, even after thirty-one years, were very difficult to write. Though I was not shocked or surprised at being let go before two of their pets, who had less plant (seniority) than I, it was hard to swallow. I thought of the hard work and sacrifice it took to earn my four-year college degree, work my way into supervision, and make many contributions in that position, including the eighteen months that I was on "special assignment" as coordinator of the Quality of Work Life process.

There were many in the corporation who, because of their performance in the QWL position, were promoted in their respective plants to seventh level positions and above, including one person who eventually became a plant manager of the motor plant next door. Another of my acquaintances in corporate communications attained staff level in communications at the Buick Division.

The assistant department head told me that I was the one to go due to my appraisal and not because I was a bad supervisor. You may recall that I had a very difficult time trying to get my general supervisor to get my appraisal completed, and when he finally did, he gave me a "good—competent" rating with the full 3.5 percent merit pay increase that went with it. At the time I thought it was no big deal, but as fate would have it, he rated his two pets as "outstanding," so they were spared at least for this round of cuts.

Most of those involved, including the two pets and others in the supervisory group in our shop, could hardly make eye contact with me when I left the office.

Amazingly, this assistant department head used my year and

a half as QWL coordinator against me, saying, "You were on special assignment for eighteen months, and I realize it takes time to get into the flow of the shop." Again, I was the one working weekends and holidays alone on the second shift while I was on that special assignment. I was never totally out of touch with the shop and with the tooling changes of the time. Even more astonishing was the fact that I had been back in the shop for almost two years since returning from the QWL special assignment.

The very next day, the assistant department head held a mandatory supervisors' safety meeting. The subject of the meeting was "safety in school areas." We were handed a sheet that read, "All supervisors are reminded that they should drive with utmost care in the vicinity of schools, now that the children have concluded their summer vacations." It was hard for me to believe that with all the hazards our employees and supervisors faced in our shop and in the production areas, all he could come up with was to watch for the kids when school begins.

During the weeks after I was notified of my termination, everyone in management avoided me as much as possible. It was and is my opinion that most of my colleagues were simply uncomfortable with the fact that I was the first to go. And all I could think about was how I would be able to take care of my wife and two young daughters, along with a mortgage payment. All of this would be problematic when my compensation stopped. I had been fortunate to have worked rather steadily for eighteen years at GM, but this was new territory for me and my family.

I called my contact in Flint, the director metallurgy at the Buick foundry. He was shocked that I was to be let go and asked me to send him my resume. I called him again a week later on September 11, 1981, and I was encouraged when he told me he had put up my résumé at a staff meeting. He said there was "much interest" and that there was a place for me at Buick if I wanted it. On the twenty-eighth, I talked to him again, and he told me he was working on setting up an interview for me.

Thirteen calendar days had passed since my notification of separation when I ran across the general supervisor who had written the appraisal that hurt me after I had to hound for months to get him to do it. He said that he had just heard of my separation and that he wanted to talk to me before I left the plant. The nerve this guy had, lying and denying right to the bitter end.

Finally, on the September, 29, 1981, I was informed that I would not have an opportunity in the Buick organization. The Buick facility was in the same shape as we were in, and they were trying to figure out who they would have to cut next, not who to hire.

So there I was, eighteen years of service to General Motors Corporation, most of it on the second shift. I had spent a five-year apprenticeship in patternmaking. I had earned a two-year Tool and Die Design diploma at Erie Community College in night school and a Bachelor of Science degree from Buffalo State College. And while in the ranks of supervision, I had been chosen to lead and coordinate the corporation's Quality of Work Life process for our plant. All this only to be the first supervisor to be let go from our group *and* with no placement anywhere in the corporation. Incidentally, I was the only one in our department's supervision group, aside from our department head, with a college degree.

In 1982 (the exact date is not clear), the Tonawanda Metal Casting Plant was completely shut down and razed with nothing remaining to remind anyone of the great years and of the thousands of lives that were affected by a total mismanagement of a business by a corporate giant.

GM Plans to Close Iron-Casting Plant In Tonawanda, N.Y.

By a WALL STREET JOURNAL Staff Reporter

DETROIT—General Motors Corp. said that it will begin phasing out operations at a large, aging foundry in Tonawanda, N.Y., and that it expects to close the plant by next June.

The auto maker also said that the continuing trend toward smaller, lighter cars may require further cuts in its iron-casting capacity. GM has four other iron foundries—two in Michigan, one in Illinois and one in Ohio.

The closing of the Tonawanda foundry will eliminate jobs currently held by 1,250 employees, GM said. An additional 880 workers are on indefinite layoff at the foundry.

GM said it decided to close Tonawanda after an internal study showed that it will have significant excess capacity for iron castings even if auto sales recovery sharply. Company officials declined to disclose either GM's current or projected casting needs.

Tonawanda apparently is the least efficient of GM's iron foundries. The company described it as having an "old, less efficient hot-metal distribution system, a congested equipment layout and worn and obsolete melting and molding equipment."

GM said it will continue to study its four remaining foundries to see where other cuts might be made in its capacity.

Courier Express Article on Tonawanda Metal Casting Plant Closing.

More Plants May Close, GM Chairman Warns

10/13/81

NEW YORK (UPI) — General Motors board chairman Roger B. Smith, facing a new round of union bargaining next year, predicts more U.S. auto plants will close unless labor costs are controlled.

"The lights in U.S. auto plants have been going out all over America — extinguished by high labor costs," Mr. Smith said in a speech to the Financial Executives Institute Monday.

"The price is too high for us and it's too high for our employees," Mr. Smith added. "Remember, the ultimate price of non-competitive labor costs is jobs."

Current contracts between the United Auto Workers union and GM, Ford and Chrysler expire Sept. 14, 1982, with major bargaining expected next summer. However, both industry and union officials already have begun to lay the groundwork for the talks.

Mr. Smith cited Transportation Department figures that show American automakers have closed or have announced closure of more than 20 facilities, affecting 50,000 workers. In many cases, he said, the jobs were permanently lost.

"Unless we get a handle on excessive labor costs in our industry, there will be more plants shutting down — and more auto industry jobs going offshore," Mr. Smith said.

"Because of our long lead times, important business decisions affecting General Motors' future — and our employees future — are being made every day, based on present circumstances," he said.

"We can't wait till next year to start our discussions," Mr. Smith added. "We need to address the labor cost problem now, before too many more jobs are lost."

Mr. Smith said GM's labor costs are currently 80 percent higher than those of Japanese automakers and also 80 percent higher than the average costs for all of American manufacturing.

"All of this adds up to one simple fact of life," Mr. Smith said. "If General Motors is to continue to have viable operations here in North America, and if we are to continue to maintain a high level of employment in the United States, then we and the unions are going to have to sit down together."

He said any agreement that would help correct the labor-cost disparity "could send positive signals throughout the economy."

Courier Express Article that GM May Close More Plants.

It is upsetting to me that both parties of our government and presidents of the United States would be getting involved in late 2008 and into 2009 to bail out this same mismanaged corporation with our tax dollars. This should never have taken place and was not necessary to save GM or the auto industry. The real goal was to save the United Auto Workers' pension and health care plans, all of which were insolvent.

CONCLUSION

With all of my options exhausted within the General Motors Corporation, and because the state of the US economy was very poor in 1981, I was very concerned about what the future held for me and my family. Even though my résumé went out to several employment agencies, I was not getting any calls for interviews. It was eerily quiet as the economy continued to tank.

I also sent a résumé to the manager of technical service at the Ashland Chemical Company's Foundry Products Division in Dublin, Ohio. I took this action early in the summer of 1981 when I was covering for a vacationing pattern service supervisor. Ashland Chemical Company was a major supplier of resins, oils, and alloys to our casting plant. They also were assisting us with a changeover to the cold-box method of core making, so a technical service representative with Ashland was in our plant to assist us with the system conversion.

During a conversation with him, I discovered that his background was very similar to mine, so I asked him, "Since I will be out of a job shortly, do you know if Ashland would be looking to hire anyone in the technical service group"? He told me they only considered folks with a four-year degree. I told him that I did have a degree. He gave me his manager's contact information on the back of his business card. The next day, I sent my résumé to his manager. It was a classic situation:

the hard work of earning my degree intersected with a possible opportunity for employment. Some would call it luck.

Since I did not hear anything from the Ashland Chemical Company in June, July, August, or early September of 1981, I dismissed them as a viable employment opportunity. What I didn't know was that since our plant was such a large account for the Ashland, they made it a practice not to "steal" employees from their customers, especially large accounts such as the casting plant. As soon as my employment termination was public knowledge, I received a call from Ashland's personnel department. This was huge on so many levels.

Arrangements were made so that as soon as I completed my last week at the plant, they would fly me to Columbus, Ohio, and then on to their headquarters in Dublin for interviews with four managers, lunch included. I flew out and back on a Tuesday in early October 1981 and in the early evening on Friday of the same week, I took a call from the personnel director telling me that they wanted to offer me a position as technical service representative in the Foundry Products Division.

This was to be a life-changing event. It involved pulling up stakes and leaving our hometown and relatives, selling our home and relocating, so I asked if I could have the weekend to discuss it with my family. That was fine with him.

I remember calling my mom that evening and telling her of the situation. She said that my dad—the tough guy, as she put it—was teary eyed upon picking up on the conversation. It was a difficult weekend, but when all the dust settled, we decided that this was a great opportunity for a new start. I called Ashland on Monday morning; we discussed the numbers, which were surprisingly generous; and I was told to expect a package of employment paperwork within a few days.

I was surprised to be allowed to stay in town until we sold our home (that would never have happened in GM). We also had to find and purchase a home in the Worthington, Ohio area as well as research schools for our two girls.

My termination and hiring were an example of how the General Motors Corporation was getting rid of skilled and talented employees who in many cases were being hired by well-run companies preparing for the eventual turnaround in the economy.

In April of 2012, I read an article in our daily newspaper in Charlotte, North Carolina, that GM was anticipating a difficult time meeting the demand for their vehicles in the spring and summer because of limited plant facilities and difficulty hiring skilled employees. Now whose fault was that? I would bet that their corporate structure is not much different from what it was decades ago.

What did they use the 49.5-billion-dollar bailout for if not manufacturing plants and skilled employees? In my opinion, and that of others, the majority of that money went to shore up the beleaguered United Auto Workers' underfunded pension and health care plans.

My first year with the Ashland Chemical Company included travel to customers' operations throughout the eastern United States. After one year in the technical service position, I was recommended for and promoted to a sales position with a territory covering Michigan, which I worked very hard for the next four years.

By early 1986, the US casting industry was being eviscerated by, you guessed it, the continued assault by Japanese manufacturers. Having knowledge of the fact that casting facilities across the country were closing by the scores each week, I decided to give entrepreneurship a shot. This was a very difficult decision for my wife and me, but much more so for our daughters. Once the details of this new chapter were worked out, we moved once again, this time to the Charlotte, North Carolina area where we have lived since 1986.

Once I got the business ownership bug out of my system, I sold it in 1990 and went to work for two large manufacturing companies for the next ten years. Then, early in 2002, I made another career change, jumping into residential real estate, where I experienced a great run through 2011. I left the business in late 2011 because the "hope and change" was not working for me.

Even though leaving the automobile industry late in 1981 was difficult, my family and I would have missed out on so much. Also, working in the GM corporate environment for another fifteen to twenty years before I could retire would have been very difficult if the environment remained as it was. In addition, my daughters would not have experienced life outside the western New York area. Rather, they got a taste of Michigan, Ohio, and finally the North Carolina, where my wife and I and our two daughters have resided and have been very happy since 1986.

The downside, of course, is that after eighteen years of service in GM, I did not receive any medical coverage once I hit the magic age, and my monthly check from GM would be and is extremely small compared to the folks I worked with that chose not to improve their lot and just put in the time punching the clock. Many of these employees were placed in other plants and eventually retired with full benefits.

Am I bitter? No. Did I miss not being involved in the automobile manufacturing business? Without a doubt yes, even with all the grief that went with it.

Back during the turmoil of the late seventies, General Motors Corporation stock was selling in the mid- to high nineties, and many employees were buying stock for years in the Salaried Stock Purchase Plan so they and their families would have a more comfortable retirement. However, when GM and our plant were quickly sliding into the abyss, the stock price was also plummeting and caught many folks who were approaching retirement flatfooted. They woke up one day to see their GM stock priced in the forties then thirties, thereby crushing their retirement dreams.

Then in 2009, after more than thirty years of what I believe to be gross mismanagement of their product lines and the cumulative effects of years of irresponsible collective bargaining agreements as well as the poor state of the economy, General Motors Corporation found itself in a financial bind requiring that they ask for federal government assistance. In my opinion, their massively underfunded pension and health care liabilities played a major role in this unnecessary action.

Rather than GM going through a corporate reorganization to get its house in order, the federal government (taxpayers) bailed them out to the tune of 49.5 billion bucks to shore up the UAW's underfunded benefits and build the Volt electric car. No new plants opened to produce products desired by the consumer, because most of the money was being used to prop up the pension funds and retiree health accounts. While the bond holders and taxpayers were being shafted, the government and the UAW became owners of the General Motors Corporation. Don't they do that in China, Russia, and Venezuela?

Finally, after all of that bailout nonsense, with the federal government's blessing, General Motors began rolling Chevy Volts off the production lines to appease the environmentalists and Obama's alternative energy agenda. The problem is that it requires government subsidies (taxpayer funds) of 7,500 dollars per vehicle to promote sales, and the folks still are not buying them.

Unbelievably, General Motors stock remained mired at around twenty-five dollars per share through late 2012, when its stock offering after the bailout was thirty-three a share. This is a far cry from its highs of three or four decades ago, and General Motors cannot place the blame for its current issues on the Japanese this time around.

In early December 2012, GM announced it had made a *net*

profit of around 5 billion dollars, and the question is, when will the US taxpayer get paid back for the government's 49.5 billion bailout?

By mid-December 2012, the US Treasury announced it would sell all remaining GM stock, as the automaker would be initially buying back 200 million shares at $27.50 per share. At that price, the government (taxpayers) would take a loss. And financial experts are saying it must now sell the remaining 300 million shares over the next twelve to fifteen months at a price of nearly 70 dollars per share *to break even*. Folks, don't hold your breath.

The American people would sure like to see the accounting on all of this rather than have someone like Timothy Geithner spew his nonsense. Folks need to follow the bailout money trail between GM, Chrysler, and our federal government and not let the money fall into the abyss of union slush funds, free phones and service, and Obamacare funding.

I sincerely hope, for the sake of thousands of union and non-union employees and their families that General Motors continues to improve its product lines, to be financially responsible, and to produce products that the consumer wants so their current employees do not have to go through what tens of thousands have had to endure over the past forty years. There is no reason GM could not be the number-one automobile manufacturer on the planet.

God bless the United States of America.

ABOUT THE AUTHOR

 In 1964 I began my career in General Motors as an apprentice metal patternmaker (model maker), became a journey man in this skilled trade, and for five years worked as a supervisor in that department.

In 1974 I graduated from the New York State University College at Buffalo with a degree in Criminal Justice while employed at the Chevrolet Metal Casting Plant in the Buffalo, New York area.

Following my "separation" from General Motors in October of 1981, I was hired by the Ashland Chemical Company Foundry Products Division based in Columbus, Ohio. Along with that my family and I endured our first relocation and left the Buffalo, New York area for good.

In 1986 we relocated for the second time when I resigned from the Ashland Chemical Company and moved to Charlotte, North Carolina where I bought and opened up a franchised printing business. Then in 1990, after three very difficult years building up the business we decided to sell it at which point I went back into manufacturing. In 2002, after returning from a two year experiment on the Gulf coast of Florida, I began a career as a residential real estate broker until retiring from it in October of 2011.

The material for this book was in three spiral notebooks put away in an attaché case for many many years and, about the time of the Obama automobile bailouts, I made up my mind to write the book so the reader could get a unique perspective about how things were in G.M. back when I was with them. One would hope that the management culture at General Motors would have improved over the past three decades but I wouldn't hold my breath with the Chevy Volt fiasco being a prime example of mismanagement.